TICK

Questions 1–32 from pages 56–59 of SEXUAL ABUSE –
THE CHILD'S VOICE, Madge Bray, Jessica Kingsley
Publishers, London, 1991.

1. Oh, my goodness me, are you a very, very big policeman?

Who frightened you? Who hurt you?

Far too young to be protecting someone, yet that's the obvious answer: What's inside that little stupid twitch and dodge? Who taught you to do that? Why would you protect the person who hurt you? So they could do it again? Does that overwhelming self-destroyed – what? Instinct? – at such a brand new age make any real fucking sense? Were you born this fucked up? How does all that fear soak down into those brittle bones that fucking quick?

They take care of you, don't they? They protect you. And you already know that there's nothing else outside? Nothing better? What else can you do? Is that it? There's so many more good hours than bad, aren't there? Warm times, I guess, when you play and when you show off to the audience that chose you.

You do what they say. And they haven't told you what's bad yet. Right? It doesn't hurt; really, does it? And all the time passes away so quickly. Into baby time. Into what you do whenever you want time.

No one really did hurt you, did they? Why would they want to? You're too pretty, too perfect, too valuable. Aren't you?

Don't worry, sweetheart, everything's fine. The policeman won't hurt you. Do you even know what that fucking means? No one would let him. Right? You don't get hurt, do you? Not here. Not when you know how really safe you really must be. Like you are. Always. Always have been, right?

Tell the old lady to shut up. Tell her to stop saying stupid things and stop making such rotten filthy talk come out of her horrible ugly smirking mouth. She shouldn't smile when she's being so mean to you, should she? She shouldn't like it. She shouldn't lean that way, manipulate that way, dress that classless way. She likes to make you frightened and cry. With her ugly mouth. All the paint on her war mouth and on her ageing hiding face. Look at her.

As close as she looks at you. Size her up the same way she packages you back to you. Tell her to shut it. Tell her to leave the baby alone.

A. WHAT IS IT ABOUT CHILDREN THAT YOU FIND SO ESPECIALLY APPEALING?

A1. *I flipped through the photos in a John Douglas book and found two new photos of Amber Hagerman. The first one –* Amber Hagerman with her brother at what turned out to be the last Christmas of *her life – came courtesy of Richard Hagerman. The second photo was a full page reproduction of the Crime Stoppers Reward poster.*

2. Are you the biggest policeman in the whole world?

Someone stuck something small and dirty inside her. Something that wasn't made to fit. Up into her. Something dirty as far as it would jam until that someone thought they'd better not push anymore. They thought they should stop. Before he ruptured the tiny gutty insides to a new hard faint. Maybe she'd die. When he only wanted to fuck her. When he didn't really even want just that. He wanted – right then, right now – to have his oily ethnic finger bent straight inside of her. To squeeze it in between the peach slit centered inside a new fresh small warm girl's body. A bendable struggling little girl's body that you could pick up and spin and make laugh and twist and toss and giggle and rub and pull and pry and split into giving just a wee bit more, there, there, and push and waste wash and shit and piss all over itself against itself. Very small. And too tight, too fused to enter. To violate. To penetrate into fitting nicely like it's fucking supposed to, you wretched fucking slut.

Just his crooked tired finger scraping inside the baby body like a bent up aged adult long dirty finger inside another giving speeding adult's sweating asshole. It'll feel the same minus the knowledge and acceptance. You'll see. You'll grow into it. Around it. And the condescension. And the waiting. The braying. Saving. Spending. Hoping.

Praying. Begging.

Are you in?

Is that good?

Do you like that?

This way or how about this? I've been saving this idea all this time, just for this night.

They kiss. They moan deep and listen to the next steps TV taught them to surprise, first, and win, second, and talk about, third, forever.

Simpering orgasm solicitude. Their lies – immediate and easy – about their mistakes and losses and special new fucking dog plans.

Do you want it deeper?

Can you take that, can you, whore, you want it all the way, do you?

A2. *Underneath her badly xeroxed face, under her $75,000 face:* AMBER HAGERMAN, WHITE FEMALE AGE 9, 4'6, 80 LBS, BLUE EYES, SHOULDER LENGTH HAIR, WHITE SHIRT WITH MULTI-COLOR HAND PRINTS, PINK PANTS, BROWN SHOES, BLACK AND WHITE BOW IN HER HAIR.

3. Are you very strong?

You're very gentle, aren't you? You're very tiny and careful and you need someone between you and those who are much bigger than you.

But – no one wants to hurt you, dear. The world isn't like that. And you're too young to hear about that, aren't you? You need to be kept – saved – innocent. Just like you are, just like you were. You need to be fed innocence. Untouched. Cradled. Owned. For as long as we can – and that, then, is the true tragedy here. Sweetheart. For someone like you who's too young to hear all this. This garbage that shouldn't be part of your wet staid personality. Yet. Never. You shouldn't have any of this inside anywhere in you.

You don't have to be real yet. You don't have to be strong. You don't have to put on a happy face if you don't want to. You shouldn't even know the difference

between your safety and their pleasure and the beast with the crinkled mouth lines and old scrunched forehead and pointy pink fingernails and age-spots and slippery baby talk should just shut her fucking noisy yawn and leave all those mean evil hating ideas out of your hairless soft ears and shrinking brain.

You're not old enough to wear make-up like that. You don't want to; not out like that, do you? If we dressed you up – would you look like her? All ageing and drooping and sunken and bloated and pinched like that? No. You're too good for all of this, my special sweetheart. You're too good for all of it. You don't pretend to be strong for anyone. You're just a tiny girl. And don't be fooled by what she says: You don't have to like anyone just 'cause they're strong. Just because they're bigger than you. You can be as frightened as you feel the need to be and you don't heve to listen to this cloying watery sugar shit anymore.

You're worth way too much.

A3. *I turned to the index and found only one page listed after her name: 155.* <u>Hagerman, Amber, abduction and murder of, 155.</u>

4. Have you come to help us, then, because we rang down to the police station for some help a minute ago?

It was a dirty finger. A finger with wet dirt from being sopped into his mouth first and then rubbed around his pervert lips dripping with drool and spit and wet milky excitement.

Like a skinny little cock'd blow-job. The way you see post paid whores on porn do it. You poke it in your mouth and get it all soaking wet. You tongue from the inside and taste, hot, the worker's dirt, the open piss hole, the honest rimmed filth of that thing that goes somewhere else better and then you – kiss – it out. To paint the whore hole. Drying up the cordial grease and slathering it with new muddied sweat and talking stink. This'll fit fine,

honey: The whore says as she looks at the $200, $300, $500 or so. This'll all be over – acting included – in well under an hour.

You insert your measly finger into the porno fuck first. Your wife, the mother of your child, the one that wanted it worse than you, her fault, your girlfriend. The mawkish lump you probed as introduction. The stumbling cocksucker you tasted with your mouth then wanted to stick a finger inside, lightly, since you're used to feeling guts with your digits rather than your tongue and your cock.

Into the pillow.

Into the wall in an alley.

Into the popcorn couch in front of the always on TV. A rented motel room. A hard wood floor. A nursery carpet. A department store rest room. The marital bed. The steamy studio apartment. The drunk, the excuses, the yearning, the stupidity, the quelled, the paid, the protected.

You wet your finger and slide it past that meat that parts queasily in nature and gives in warm and rigid and soft and black.

Sometimes an audio cassette will be just the right enough. No face, bites, ass, nesting instinct or performing horse tricks.

A4. *It's one fucking paragraph. However, it turned out to be a comparison to the abduction, rape and murder of Polly Klaas which was covered at length.*

5. Do you catch people who hurt children?

Do you remember what you used to look like?

The old pig with the mouth all over the small growing mind of the littlest pained raped child starts to lock and suck. She tastes what she was and swallows all that grown up cum: pooled in the tiny deepening crevices of twisted grey matter clogging up the stupid happiness impulses that spark playtime.

The old pig doesn't forget. Her job, here with the

cop and the notes for the already advanced book, is completely dependent on this little baby's penis stuffed mouth and digit'ed cunt.

Do you remember what you looked like?

Do you remember what it tasted like? And how much better you can make it taste now – how much brighter the colors are now when you paint them over and over again until, because you have to stop when the pigments slush into black smeared mud, you have to start brand new all over again. The same painting. The same cartoon. The newer promise. The refreshing new twist. The exciting fresh start just after the cheap neon garage sale.

A5. *Another photo of a smiling cutie with barrettes in her hair:* Cassandra Lynn "Cassie" Hansen was abducted from church in St. Paul, Minnesota, on November 10, 1981. Her body was found in a dumpster the next morning.

6. Well, are you very strong? Are you very, very strong?

You fingerfuck her. Like you fingerfuck any teenage date. You slip just one finger inside of her. And, since it's dreamier when you close your eyes, you do. With your finger then worming your way up the entire other of a stranger's body it becomes a – say – four-year-old baby child. A small girl body. A little toddler struggling her smile around full sentences and absolute need. Whose cunt is a better cunt? The date with her age and lapses and make-up and adulthood coming tits and hips and lips and jobs or the child she once was ironed down deep inside beneath the survivalist praise for a wonderous brand of god-given innocence. Which trade-marked flavor of innocence do you dig through with only one finger first?

You necessarily hold back. You learn. You go slow. You register.

How can you possibly let me do this to you?

A6. Hansen, Cassandra Lynn "Cassie", abduction and murder of, 99–115, profile in, 101–6.

7. How strong are you? Can you show us?

You compare. I'll show you.

I started doing it with hookers. I was so low by the time I started it seemed like the only logical progression. Or, at least, a next step. I had sunk from getting sucked by them to asking – paying – them to remove their shirts and then masturbating myself. I didn't want any part of them to touch me. I didn't want them to be working on me, manipulating my cock, or performing on me. My hard-on was fixed before I laid eyes on their tar stained uniqueness. I cummed in mine. But soon that fell through as well. I looked at their ugly withered bruised bodies and wanted less. Those flat stretched hog jowls, liver lips and beaten arms. I see them on HBO. Their children at home and their stunted conversations; I'd had them all before. The crimes in their stalking forests and their sisters dumped in garbage cans. I didn't have to squat so pathetically low to get it again and again. So, I started to offer them more money. I always offered them more money. But now I wanted something more for it. And I asked. Can I put my finger inside your vagina. Can I see your ass and can I put my finger in it, please. Cunt, pussy, butthole. Words that reeked of their yellowed minds. Abutted by their very specific African sensibility: Can I put my finger in. Not stick. Put. Place.

I let them tell me the new amount. How much more money do you want – exactly – to allow me to put my finger inside your vagina? And in your ass. I never haggled. Almost always it was $50.00 which is way too expensive and just fine by me.

You can put anything you want in there.
Are you clean? Did you wash?
Just one finger.
I ain't gonna get all wet that way.
You sure y'all just want your finger in there?
Go on Honey, you stick it in.
Ain't nothin' goin' in my asshole.
Motherfucker.
You want me to turn around?

Did you get yo' nut?

I ain't doing nothin' afters. That's all you payin' fo'.

Let me see your fingernails.

If you be motherfuckin' careful.

I've even wrapped a condom around my finger before penetrating a nigger cunt. This probably being more my problem than hers.

I don't care if they buck, moan or sleep. I don't like them wiggling their tongues like snakes as they watch my embarrassed face and I prefer their tops on, covering their browned tits and completely hiding their black cow lick nipples.

Is this where the baby came from? The one addicted and quaking and crying from crack? Is this where your brother and his basketball buddies slipped their jungle loads into you? Where your first street whore fuck slimed his condom'd whites into you?

How many fingers before this one?

How many fingers until you feel it?

I was a meat packer. My whole body stunk like offal. I struggled to hold on to wet sliding fat purple cow livers grabbed from the bottom of huge cardboard plastic lined barrels soaked in thick black blood. If you didn't want to drop the heavy meat into the sawdust and shavings and boot dirt, you dug your fingernails deep into the squishy weight and held it away from your hardly clean white meat frock. Flanks – white and deep red and warm hunks of poundage – had to have the cow shit cleaned off them. Tumors and noids and muscles had to be incised – the smell and the phantom texture penetrating your gut and staining you for the bulk of your weekend.

I fingered other assholes before hers.

I frigged the asshole of an AIDS death when he asked me to.

There's these old timers: A grandpa who comes into the peep booths I mine. He saunters past me straight into the tight black wall corner. He turns back around towards me and drops into a squat. He's here to suck up cock immediately and make his submissive position as clear

as dog.

He helped me with my pants not saying a word. He had placed in my hand a handful of gold tokens for the screen ambiance and the red "on" light outside. He yanked down my pants, shimmied down my boxers and bobbed at my flaccid penis.

I prefer a condom.

At the time I preferred to keep my cock soft as long as possible. Now I try to show hard and finish quick.

He licked and sank: on to my balls, my piss hole, my choad, my jock itch, with his hands on my bare ass.

"Did you fuck any children today?" he sneered from down below my waist.

"Fuck off..."

"Did you – did you fuck any kids today with this? With this?"

"The fuck's wrong with you?" Cops don't suck cock, hopefully. They don't berate you while they hold on to your balls and shaft, certainly. Some faggots forget where they are. Want to take their phone sex games out with them. They watch too much porno. Read too many books. And risk getting their fucking faggot faces kicked in. Then: "Do you know who I am?"

"Can I have some of it?"

I pushed farther into his mouth, choking him. He gagged and garbled and sputtered back only to breathe and lick at my glans.

"I want to taste those kids. Those children you fuck with this. Give them to me." And he headlonged into it.

"Shut up and finish" I told him. He groaned. "I hate faggots like you. Old man."

He pumped at his meal worm cock in the dark. I watched down at his head under my belly. At his faggot hunting. His snake hands pushed into my loose ass and around my legs up to my chest and around my waste and hips and thighs.

"Jesus fucking christ. You want to taste those little punks. You want to swallow up all that blood?"

"Yes, please, sir, yes, please."

A7. The medical examiner found no evidence that she'd been sexually assaulted, though small traces of semen and several pubic hairs were discovered on one thigh of her navy blue tights.
(Journey Into Darkness, John Douglas & Mark Olshaker, Scribner, 1997, page 100.)

8. Can you lift that?

I'll show you.

I leaned into his mouth. I took my right hand and steadied myself on the wall across, just above my head. My left hand leaned into the oher corner with him between. On me.

Can you stand still?

I had to hold on. I balanced myself on my arms and queened wholly into his sucking slurping swallowing face. My hands in the greasy smear inside the hot box closet with the TV and the cheap porn and the cum dollops and this geriatrically hot AIDS mouth.

His hands scurried from my balls to my sweaty crack, brushed his filthy asshole fingers near mine.

I pushed harder down his throat and told him to watch it.

"Knock it off."

More licks and now strokes.

"How old were they? How old was the little baby you fucked today?"

"Young. Too young for you, old man."

"I can taste it. I can taste that little cunt. Mmmmm. There – there it is. Mmmmm." His old dad tongue lolling and spreading his stink all over my fat reddening thick cock head.

"Inside."

Which he took to mean: more sucking.

"Harder."

My sac and his wash, my shaft and his yank and glide, my hatred and his swallowing.

You have to be careful now.

"Mmmmm. Did you kill her?"

11

"Shut the fuck up. Finish."

"You did, I know you did."

"You don't ...fucking.. Shut it now."

I wanted to fuck this mouth more than ever suddenly. He'd won. By far. And I wanted to cum with his mouth slurping murder ministrations all over me. But I'm no good with fiction and I'm shit with talking fantasies. I wanted his child killing mouth to bring me off immediately on some specific cunt raped and throated little piggie like Amber Hagerman. I pulled out of his stretched and soaked face and started masturbating inches back into his mouth.

"You see that? You fuck your daughter with that mouth? Did you?"

He was pumping. Snaking his gross tongue out at my cock and then up at my face. His shave, splotches, baldness, wrinkles, gray pimpled chalk pale complexion.

"Yes. Yes I did. I fuck her with your dick."

"Not with mine, pal. You got that thing there – that fucking beast, did you stick that thing in her?"

"Yeah – a lot. All the fucking time." And back to pillorying.

"What did it feel like. What does your daughter's stretched out baby cunt feel like?" I grabbed the base of my cock and yanked my balls harder than he could.

"Like your dick. I can taste her on your cock."

I held his head and pumped into his old man head like I would have fucked his daughter as per his own instructions.

"Can I fuck her? Will you let me?"

I held his head tight. Groans from deep while his tongue fought to lick, first, perform, second, and breathe, third.

"Can I fuck her. How old is the little cunt? How old is the little bitch – your fucking cunt wife's ugly baby." I wanted to smash his head with my hands and cut his throat with the torn shards of the TV screen. My balls in his face. My cock in his head. Him pulling himself off below me, in the filth and the dark and the safety.

"How tight is her little cunt, you faggot."

A8. *From the same paragraph:* <u>Abrasions across her chest</u> <u>indicated that another belt had been used as a restraint</u> <u>around her upper body.</u>

9. Oh, my goodness, you must be strong, and can you lift this?

I turned to the screen. Away from his toilet.

You must be strong. What is your current T-cell count? Your viral load? When did you first suspect you were HIV positive? Do you know how you got it? Who gave it to you? Have you confronted him? Do you hate him? You do understand that this is no longer a death sentence, right?

Do you still practice safe-sex?

Do you still take it in the ass?

Do you believe in re-infection?

Do you let strangers cum in your mouth?

Do you like the way nonoxynol tastes?

What about the toxins? Can you try and make it to the bathroom on your own this morning?

Would it have been rude to not wet my finger a second time before sticking it back in again. All that rank meat, that chewed blacker than bile gristle and gluey liver guts. Her piss slit. Her crack baby hole. That squashing soft suffering head being slid, forced, dropped out of that spread forgotten crumbling seething nigger sewer.

How low did it get before it just stopped.

Those quick trembles of nausea started from what act, exactly?

What do you hold dear? What do you keep safe? What says yours to you?

Your mother helped hard to raise you because your father worked all day into night. He paid your selfish bills and she pat your spreading head. She made the phone calls and hoped to set up your future. And you repaid her with getting sex slung AIDS before your thirtieth birthday. Older than most. Old enough to know better. To have chosen something better.

Did you tell her?

barely look. I back up.

"Can I go again."

Her ratted lungs hiss and her talons extend to my forearm to postion my finger back to the nest, quickly, to get all this sick fuck stupidity over with. She pulls at my pants to ball up my straining hard-on. To check if she has a chance to finish up even sooner. And maybe safer. And the less of this dirty pig all the better. I am this low.

Another spit to my finger. Like you should do when you're counting lots of stranger's dollar bills. You don't lick your finger after flipping through all that coke and germs.

Her cunt reeked like knots of old washing left over hard hot liquor soaks. Vomit. Roaches. Strains. Tears. The kind that thinks it deserves a little more only when it's slightly sober.

"Is that all you want to put in there?"

Another twenty bucks so I can finish inside her mouth. That pressed and drooped blackened corpse face that belongs behind bars and guards looks best when watching my fat belly and balls rather than my decidely unsteady face.

A9. *And:* The six-year-old had been scratched and beaten about the head and face.

10. Well, I think you must be a very strong policeman. Can you lift that?

Women experience HIV differently than men. Drugs create different changes and effects. Women die faster.

I could offer to pay the open lump in Ziagen. I should show her my warning sign. I should ask her:

"What kind of drugs are you going to buy with this money?"

The fished rank from her hollow bucket cunt is less natural than the fished rank of other parasites. The fished rank from both sets is less natural than the hard bite fished rank of AZT and more left all over my spreading hand.

A10. *The next book John Douglas and Mark Olshaker published had, on the very first page of the photo section, an absolutely incredible shot of Dee. Her mother was in another shot, below her, smiling:* in happier times. Since Dee's death she has struggled heroically to put her life in order and fight for victims' rights.

11. Are you very, very strong?

Why should she take the drugs that'll keep her living? Why should she – honestly – waste all the money and time in toxic stutter? The recreational drugs make more sense. To die without being bored while infecting and flaking away all the extra days these rich cocksuckers have. To enjoy yourself by yourself in yourself. With god.

But logic doesn't fit comfortably inside those medicinally caulked craters. Another day is another day and all the promises that have been piling up must be due incredibly soon.

My finger tastes like salmon synthetics. It smeared meat delivery van steering wheel over my own heavy drugs with crumpled porno money and the meat I grab and cut and tie for at least eight years now.

And I lick it again. To go back deeper. This time: I taste her. All that sinking filth. All that disease plus. And the sexual question is sudden and brutal: Is there more pain inside that than just pure and simple hideous loss. Her ugliness. Her turpitude. Degeneracy. And if there's a game here, a will to power, a faggy deconstruction: Am I lower than her? Than it? And even lower now that I've done something dirtier than pay her for what she has. Had. And the pit of my gut swells with acid and pepto bismal and salt and chemo and all her bacteria and insects and silent carving death and I am pushed to believe that, culturally, I've done all of this to myself and she's not quite that sad.

I have to get my finger wet so I can fit it back in between the folds of her faultless massacred body.

I get my finger wet by sucking on it with my mouth and tongue and teeth and caps so I can enter her blacking body as close as I possibly can for twenty fucking

nigger fucking dollars.

My knuckles register her flabby given adipose ass and her toilet brush wire bush. Her chafing pink brown to black welts. My spittle. My spit will taste back like her for years now. Like some hasidic fuck who can't wash other's sins off him. Like maybe I do this to myself and what I deserve I get in the form of even more bang for my buck.

A11. *The photo of the little Dee was taken by mom Katie while the photo of mom was taken by Keith Souza, who must be her ex-husband. And Dee's dad.*

12. And do you catch naughty people who hurt children?

How else do you do it? What else can you do? You can't sit by fat and alone and pretend to simply soak it up by second-hand lies. You owe it to yourself, to your choices, to your time, to your pit.

You don't have to think he's beautiful. You don't think anyone is actually worth fucking, do you?

Your dirt has to cover their mud. Your filth has to be the degree that finally calls for the clean-up. You have to be all you are just for yourself, right? There's no sinking. Swoon in above it all and take from everything sliming down just below the velvet hem of your Wagnerian cape. And clean it up. By proving to all the its just how sick its are. And you breathe through that. You suck harder. You slurp back deeper. You taste what all the other scumbags miss. And only you'll know what separates you from the more depleted, more desperate lines standing in port authority and bug house square.

You don't get caught.

And you don't drop old like all these other wretches. Others. The rest of them.

You are not defined by them. By their stimulants and instincts and similarities and differences. Send your filth to me at my post office box. I want to see it.

A12. *Next to the special photo of special Dee holding her*

stuffed oversized cartoon doll and wearing her charming
plastic wristwatch and her silky hair in long page boy
bangs, her tiny gentle cheeks slightly sucked in:
On September 17, 1990, an adorable and loving little girl named Destiny "Dee" Souza was found by her mother, Katie, in the basement of their house in Fairfax County, Virginia.

13. And when you catch them, do you get very, very cross?

What exactly is my level?
It is the single worst thing you can do. To drag them down to your level. And make that level live. Beat and pump and rise. On in them. Through you. Clearly.
Some Thai faggot drops his jogging pants and yanks at a surprisingly thick nut brown cock. Heavy balls squeezed underneath a heavy silver metal cock ring and he wants you to pay to suck that cock and lick those hairless straining fat balls. His ass is smooth and tight and positioned for grabs and caresses more than messy angry hated fucks. But what's the difference, suddenly. A fuck is more expensive than what he'd prefer. Which is cheap, comparatively.

A13. *The next lines:* She was eight years old and had been beaten to death. Katie's sister's boyfriend, Robert Miller, was convicted of the murder.
Her hair and age and face are all Rodox. Page boy cut means Rodox.

14. And what do you do when you get very cross? Do you shout?

It's not my job.

A14. *From Obsession, John Douglas & Mark Olshaker, Scribner, 1998, page 177:*
"I wanted to see what was done to her," Katie says.

15. And do you shout very loud?

I've been reduced.

A. WHAT IS IT ABOUT THESE CHILDREN THAT YOU FIND SO PARTICULARLY APPEALING?

A15. *I barely know these cases. Even now; I've only scratched the surface of what I was given. I really know so little about what happened to them and their little bodies.*

16. Can you show us? Shout something.

What makes you a good cocksucker? Time? Lust? Professional concern? Fear? Indecision. Femalia. Testosterone. Instinct.

16A. *I think they're very cute.*

17. "Go away!" – Shout "Go away!"

How the fuck should I put myself in her place? I'm not even fucking interested. If some stupid fucking woman wants to get blasted and sloppy and then ends up naked getting fucked by someone who doesn't normally deserve such delicate favors; why should it be my job – as what? as a gentleman? – to protect her. From who? Herself? The troll? Someone who doesn't care as much as me, someone who's not as sensitive? A sucker, a cuckold, a teddy bear.

And it's her stinking mouth – her drunken trollop mouth that is asking to be stuffed. And what's the big fucking deal? One single simple fuck. And, OK, what that can lead to: death by virus, broken beer bottle, court room S/M arguments, gossip. Is it my job to protect her or not to take advantage of her? Tell me where the damage is –.

Hold this teddy bear, you tell her. And you snap a photo of her on her bed with the old brown smiling stuffed doll between her white legs. Take off your top. Lean back to the pillows and headboard. Rub your old friend fuzzy darling between your spread wide thighs. Like

you did when you were so much younger. Such a naughty brat. You did, didn't you? Did you really?

The alcohol that burns her crown blurs your words into memories and she's easily living her preteen sexual fumblings: Her tiny raw clit and ever ready friendly brown scratching post.

Tie her hair into pig-tails with strips ripped from her baby doll Gap top. The tight advertising she wore out for tonight's perfectly understood youthful pigging.

Are you too drunk to shave?

Kids today are so promiscuous, aren't they?

Tell me about your first time – when did you first become aware of your mighty sex drive?

Did it include getting fucked?

Raped?

Was it a safe female experience – do you remember if you moved at all, you filthy dead soaped fish?

Did you suck?

Do you like having piss-holes in your mouth. That hot muscle veined taste – did you imagine what it would taste like or did you focus on your beauty and mirror power as you cooed and petted and bequeathed? Trade kisses with your bathroom reflection? Make your finger hurt and your shoulder ache?

Do you understand what I'm doing? Do you mind? I like it when you pretend to be much younger.

A17. *Twenty years or so ago I purchased a book called Violence In Our Time by Sandy Lesberg. It had a huge effect on me. On my late puberty and on my tastes.*

18. Do you like little girls?

You can tell me.

A18. San Francisco, California, June 1948 – A juvenile probation officer comforts 5-year-old Sharon Steward who was found naked in a filthy closet, suffering from malnutrition. Summoned by neighbors who heard the child's continuous crying, police found a bureau jammed

against the closet door and clothes crammed beneath the door. The father was on a fishing trip and the mother had taken two of their other children to the beach.
(Violence In Our Time, Sandy Lesberg, Haddington House, 1977, page 18)

19. Are you very kind to little girls?

Has anyone ever hurt you? Deeply hurt you? When did that start? When did the memories switch from perfect to muddied? When you were how young? Your daddy or one of his friends? Has mom ever thought to sell your baby body for her last chance at some street crack? Is a fingerfuck all that happened the first time?

A19. An oversized full page shot of naked 5-year-old Sharon in black and white. Dirty and still crying, her pubic area carefully covered by the prim probation officer's arm, who reaches across to a drawer of the evil bureau. The female cop's knelt down in front of the little skinny girl, her face comfortingly close to the child's.

Naked Sharon's black hair is messy and tangled and long around her crying face. Her ribs push through her fragile chest but she doesn't look entirely Third World. She's white and hurt and neglected but not alien. She's been taken care of better than that.

20. Well, do you think perhaps you could help us; would you like to help us?

Why would someone do that? Why do you think? Just stick their finger in that clamp of yours? You wouldn't imagine someone would like doing that if you weren't going to enjoy it. Too.

Would you have preferred a cock? Something with some weight and life to it?

Is that how you cum?

From inside?

If I tell you where my hands have been today, will you be honest and tell me where your cunt has been? For

all these years? Since the very first time you had something go the wrong way. When outside saturated your inside. And you became a lousy hole. And how lucky that there's always an audience not bothered by the plebian.

I want to make you look younger.

I want to fuck something that closely fools me into you being anything other than you: Like a little you – a little girl you. Before you were just short of too old and too available and too drunk.

Why do you drink?

You can't handle it.

I don't want an apology on my answering machine the next day. I don't want to have to explain to you how it's alright and that you're not a slag and that it really is no big fucking deal.

You used a condom, didn't you?

He didn't fuck you in the ass, did he?

You don't think you're pregnant, do you?

Did he still want to fuck you even after he saw your herpe sores?

Did the end of his cock taste like the beer he's been pissing out all night?

Did you stick his finger in your mouth after he tested the swamp waters to see how wet you were. Or if he'd fit just yet. Or if you stank. If you shaved. If you were clean. If there were crabs or ointments or yeast or a rag and a plug or a slack jawed maw big enough for his worker's forearm.

Did he say please? Did you?

Did you ask for compensation?

And the next day when you tried to forget how stupid you were from underneath that eye wrenching pain and headache haze; did you understand that what you fucked and what he fucked were two entirely different creatures. That you were just any open sewer. And that what he wanted was just a little child. That you fucked a child molester who used your everything as the little sexy kidling that he would've raped if he could. Instead of you. That the cum that slides down his erection into your stripper's pubis and down into your shaved ass and across

your careful belly was child rape. As close as you'll come. But not him.

Kiss the teddy bear.

Put on the pink panties.

Wipe your make-up off and let's re-do it. Your blush, your cheeks, your used freshness, your JonBenet lips.

I hate your tits. Can't you cover them up or cut them off or something?

Turn around.

Lay flat on your stomach.

Keep your head down.

Spread your ass with your fingers and leave the fucking cunt stenched teddy bear lying in the middle of your back.

Don't say a fucking word. I don't want to hear you play the game. I don't even want to hear you say: Daddy.

It's just my finger first.

I'll tell you what you had for dinner last night.

Don't cry.

It's not worth it. It's just a finger. And I'll make sure it's lubed.

This hole is for child rapists, you understand?

Tight.

I'll keep you soft and pliable, enterable, with your lipstick.

That way I can see your child's cunt in the dark. Just like lipstick is supposed to do. Don't move. Don't buck. Don't put on a show.

I don't believe you.

How much to fuck your sister?

With lipstick all over her mouth – to show me where to stick it. How much younger is she and – did you look like her back then?

How much for just my finger?

Don't answer.

Don't slur.

Let's go get your sister. Remember that when you wake up tomorrow. When I fucked your ass – I talked

about your sister. Remember that.

A20. *Sharon is the one I remember thinking of the most back when I was masturbating the most often. 5-year-old naked Sharon was the one I thought of when I was bored in High School. I couldn't wait, it would seem, to relieve the pressure in my pants and head by fucking that photo over and over again in my mother's bathroom.*

21. Oh, good, because we've got a smashin' little girl here and we think maybe some naughty person has done something to her private parts and hurt her a lot –.

You're a very cute girl.
        You're a very cute girl with a darling little cute
face.
        Very cute.
        You have a lovely smile.
        I think you're very precious. Very cute. Very
special.
        Very beautiful.

A21. *She was more than a naked child. Her hair and nipples and legs and the tip of her boney hips. I was aware that there was so much more going on in there right from the start.*

22. Oh, good; well, what will you have to do? Will you have to get your book out and write this person's name down?

How terrible it must be to have become infected with creeping death from someone as low as this. Sex is all youth. And then all memory. And to see, when you're cleaning your store bought vegetables and fruits with bleach lest there be even the most microscopic germ or bacteria still waiting to kill you, a cock underneath a belly as ugly and fat and white as that. Again and again when trying new drains and new nucleoside analog

24

combinations: A dead cock amidst all the other condoms
and plastic gloves; cum and piss and pus-y STDs and cheap
sure-fire sleazy glory hole joints after the bars close.
Excruciatingly slow drags on hard cocks with an asshole
that takes in all the immediacy, lonliness, depression and
ageism swimming just underneath the correct amount of
alcohol, poppers, penicillin and collapsed self-esteem.

The pickings get thinner. The crowd that sharked
around you back when you were young have slowly
enveloped you as one of their own. The pulse of the place
has only changed with your view.

I spit on my hand. And then glide my slime'd palm
back and forth on his long soft shaft. I push my hand into
his fucking teenage faggot face and tell him to lick it.

That's what your cock tastes like.

When it actually tastes like my garbage gut. My ill-
health, my mono and TB cough, my bad diet, my cancer.

And my balls.

You want to suck yourself off, faggot? You like
your dick that much? You don't do this at home?

I don't kiss.

Neither do I.

You get older. You turn. Implode, collapse, give in
to yourself. After so many years of getting what you want
as easy as this and not caring about the degree of dog
asshole open and constantly available for mere quarters 24
hours a day, you've come to wear the lazy style too deep.
At this age. At this place. With this flop sweat. With these
zits. At this same spot just like all the others: No matter
where you are you acclimate easily: Urinals in Berlin and
mirrored single hiding places in Los Angeles, Rue St. Denis
in Paris, old Show World buddy booths in NY and every
nook and cranny in Chicago shit holes. It's not knowledge,
or a wide horizon, as much as an insignificant divestment
in a slow pull through one single serial lowest common
denominator.

What else can you do?
I want you to suck it.
Use your mouth.
Let me see what you got.

You are all over yourself. Whole heartedly. And this is what was bound to happen. You became you. Folded all over yourself and blubbered and tired and hungry: All the weekly cock tricks and coin games that have slabbed their secrets into your puffy flesh rubbed and fell into cellulitis and flushes and hard arteries.

"Can I put a condom on you" you hear yourself practice. As you sit below him, waiting for him to acquiesce and ask for money. Which is easiest.

There's nothing as silly as active and passive, male and female, fucker or faggot roles here, now, right?

How low they have to be to let you hog all over them. With your AIDS and hepatitis C and their condoms. How degenerate and perversely puritan they live as your perfectly healthy but slothful wheeze slides back to their asshole and up to their boney chests.

This is what you must do: Slob into them like an old father. That'll work.

A22. *She was still crying. Always crying. Her lips jutted and eyes clenched. Her naked vulnerability, her confusion and distress. Her relief. Her fear for the future. That big woman in all those clothes and her little body in none. The fucking photographer. The neighbors. The suggestion that someone cover her.*

It was the crying that I found most salient.

23. Well, and what will you do when you catch this person?

She started it. She figured she was different by dumb dint of her past. And even though she was, right now, acting exactly like all the others out there, doing exactly what all the others do in here, she paraded her simple minutes quick self as something wholly apart.

She wasn't doing it for me. I wasn't even lucky to have her here. Understand – she was explaining, talking at my hardened cock and then face, for her. She wasn't another tramp. Lumpen was outside somewhere else. She was special to herself, for herself and, sadly, apparently,

that sometimes needs to be explained.

A23. *I also concentrated on 9-year-old Antonio on the
page just before Sharon. Much thinner and more extreme:
Antonio's naked body was lying on a concrete floor in the
right hand corner of the full page shot. His ass and balls
carefully cropped out. A chain hung from the upper left
down to the floor and around his hogtied hands and feet.
A bucket near his head had to be for pissing and shitting
and puking.*

*I was in the mood for that every now and again.
But I was overly concerned that the news service told him
to lay back down for the shot. It was good that way, I
decided later, especially after seeing how KP was filmed.
However, I seemed to obsess over Sharon – who I also
expected to have been posed somewhat.*

24. How cross will you get?

"You don't want to use a condom?"

"We ain't fuckin' – it don' matter to me. I know
you don' like it – it ain't feelin' right on you."

"I'm OK. I was asking for you."

"You ain't got nuthin' do you? I ain't worried
about you, you better not be worried about me."

And then: "I ain't got nuthin' to give you you ain't
already got." Which, of course, meant she did.

I knew before I even thought about getting a
blow-job from absolutely any nigger mouth that she would
be sick. The talk here was syrup. What she said, and the
natural way she said it, was the common variety veneer of
STD worry. She wasn't that far gone, not at all desperate,
not reduced as badly as the scumbag white john who's
twisted enough to take such stupid chances for such cheap
excuses for the briefest gratification.

But inside those colorfully chosen yips slurred in
the hope that the paying dogs don't listen to anything they
don't want to hear anyways: The truth they always
manipulate when they can't own it. Forget the context.
And it is half the charm that that simple life-long equation

gets chewed down to a stump by the daily drudgery of such inept scheming fogged by recreational need. The thick nigger skin formed over those words ends up fitting so suffocatingly tight that the only one possible to fool is the beast owning the noisy hole. She hears herself intelligent. She sees herself impress. She waves and sucks and basks. And her life is complete. For, right now, she sings, for just this little while, she heats up, that it's all starting to finally work out 'cause she knows it has to. God's been listening, certainly. Why else is she here?

To insult her tattered sheen of McDonald's rest room cleanliness with the suggestion of a protective wrap that'll numb her business lips and short her expertise and shut the ugly buzzing bugs roaring through her face and gump and blood cells back into her circular self image would have made this pathetic transaction far more difficult than necessary.

"I actually like the way it feels."
"I ain't got a lot of time."
"I cum quick."
"I hope so."

A24. Isleta, Texas, June 1963 – "Whenever mother leaves the house she ties me up", 9-year-old Antonio Valenzuela told police who found the child naked and chained to a washing machine. He also told police that his mother hit him because of the way he made coffee that morning. The boy's mother was being sought on charges of child neglect and aggravated assault.
(Violence In our Time)

25. Well, I think you are probably strong enough to help us. Can you go and catch that person, then?

I put myself here.

What's the difference between the hole behind the purple liver lips, nigger tongue wags, alcoholic gum diseases, drug flattened face, dirty hair, bone stupidity and the hole propped open by faggot service, lustful complacency and soft wired romanticism?

Money.
Time.
Taste.

A25. *There were much more graphic photos. The book was a compendium of such things. My favorite chapter was CHILD ABUSE. I was fucking amazed.*

26. Oh, hang on a minute. You don't know that person's name–
Well, who knows the name? We'd better ask the little girl.

The context slams full-stop dead at the same brick wall all the time. Fuck blunt instinct and genetic lack. It's just a difficult attention span. Did these nigger beasts ever get high school hickeys on prom nights and senior mixers. I'll give it to the motherfucker one way or another. You want to fuck this pussy. This black nigger pussy. It's nice and tight and I fuck real good. What was your lilly white age when you seen your first gun? How many have you seen growing up? All of this between licks at the pursed tip of my cock and rough tugs at my balls. A roasted pig on a spit. More grease in the crackling fire. Rib tips. White bread on top of the cheap beef slab of bones and gristle covered in BBQ sauce only niggers think is spicey.
　　"You know Luther East?"
　　"um...no."
　　"Oh I see – you didn't pay for no conversation, huh?"
　　"No. It's nice. I'm fine. What's his name?"
　　"It's a school."
　　"Oh – no. On the south side?"
　　"It's a private school. I went to school there."
　　"No. I don't know it."
　　Half my capacity was trying to make sense of the shit she was dribbling to form what could, actually, be an entertaining conversation. The other half was reeling as to where her hands were in relation to my wallet or whatever she might have hidden in her clothes. This part didn't want

to be suckered; to believe that this plug waste on the end of my straining hard-on was steeped in self-esteem problems. Or bragging the way these things do on the loud sections of the exceptionally long Chicago bus routes. Proud of the fact that it can say conversation instead of conversating.

A26. *Looking back at it now, a photo of two-year-old Sonja Peterson looks remarkably like Thea Pumbroek from the photo in Tim Tate's Child Pornography.*
        Thea Pumbroeck – victim, died aged six.
(Child Pornography, Tim Tate, Methuen, 1990)

27. Oh dear, the little girl says "nope nuffink". Do you think that's the person's name? Do you know anybody called "nope nuffink"?

"Was it nice?"
        "Yeah. I loved it. I learned, boy. It was my favorite time of my life."

A27. St. Paul, Minnesota, November 1962 – Two-year-old Sonja Peterson recovers in a hospital after her father allegedly amputated her right hand at the wrist. The father, aged 27, who at first claimed the amputation was an accident, was arrested on charges of maiming.
(Violence In Our Time)

28. Well, do you know, Mr. Policeman, do you know sometimes naughty people who hurt children, they say to children that they've got to keep it a secret and not tell anybody. Did you know that?

She didn't return to gobbling her job right away. Instead she stuck her small chest out a little more; her arms back, one hand not working but steadying on the dash, the other fingernailing the hairy base of my standing glistening cock.
        "You got nice tits."
        She was simply poodle'ing for more money. All of

this was for a tip. Like some weasely waitress giving you extra whatever after you've already paid the check. I reached over and felt at her hanging hideous flesh under her t-shirt and since I 1) didn't want to go under her shirt by her pants line 2) didn't think it would work through her drooped collar and 3) didn't want to lose my erection and stride, I figured I would simply comply to the very least expected of me. I wouldn't fuck it otherwise. I wouldn't want to.

She should have removed her shirt. She should've had me finished off by now. I was still that hard. I wanted to fuck something remotely like it. I wanted all that beefy waitressing and middle class lies to be stained, momentarily, sadly, by my dripping sickness and drive. What I excrete just slips out. Burps and bubbles and farts, so near to the ailing asshole that bleeds my toilet water bright red and squeezes itself shut on the most unhealthy greasy food and chemical sludge waste.

A28. *Sonja has her tiny good hand to her big eyes. She looks very distressed. On the verge of tears and two-year-old confusion. I might find it worrying that this personally elemental book could still carry the same power. Beyond grotesque nostalgia. I don't think that's particularly healthy.*

29. Well, little girls haven't done anything wrong, have they, but sometimes these grown-ups say to children that if they tell the secret they will get into a lot of trouble.

–And maybe some person's told this little girl that she musn't say anything about it and she has to keep it a secret. But if you were to manage to get down on your hands and knees and put your ear very close to this little girl's mouth, then maybe she could whisper the secret name of the person into your ear, because you see, we could all turn round and pretend that we're not here, because we wouldn't hear the secret. Do you think you could maybe do that?

Her tiny ploys and pleases. Her banal obsequiousness and

my ice cream eating decorum. And no matter what: I paid.
No matter what: I re-infected her.

No matter what else happens. I bought everything she said and I paid for the next few days of her dreaming up new stories and thoughts and selling suggestions with just the tiniest bit of my free time.

A. WHAT IS IT ABOUT THESE LITTLE GIRLS THAT YOU FIND SO POWERFULLY ATTRACTIVE?

A29. *It's not the only thing I like – it's not the main thing.*

30. Well, goodness me, Mr. Policeman, what a lot this little girl's been able to tell you. This little girl's been such a help to you. Do you think you could go and catch this naughty person now?

"Let's finish before the cops come."

I cum quick with prostitutes. I show hard and pop messy and fast. With faggots I try and stay soft for as long as I can because I like the way that works. With cheater's hands and full blubbering lipstick slather and melanoma blotches and breezy professional stumbling I turn cumming into a two minute piss. Less. Often enough. I soak in what I don't touch and soak through everything they do. I repeat myself. I trade them drugs for their faces. Everything I understand about them is based on what little I know and like proving.

A30. *I saw the film with tiny Dutch Thea in it. I believe it was her. I was told it was. Since the little girl died of a drug overdose just after the film was made, the film became quite well known. There was quite a lot of publicity. Thus the market for it was huge.*

Which is why I'm suspicious. I'm willing to believe that what I saw was the last film with her in it – I'm told she did a few of them, actually. Anyways, that's how I remember the film I saw. All the time. That it was definitely the right film.

31. OK, will we come and see you off?

"Thank you. Wait one second. Thank you."

A31. *I've talked about all this before. To me, I look for the drug abuse and the compact life of death. It's hard not to see it. The action is always cookie cutter. It's hard not to look for more even if it's not there on the screen. It's there. Believe me.*

32. Will you be very cross?

I give her an extra ten bucks. What's worth fucking twice? Is that what you marry? What you take home and let hold you?

What does your wife turn into in so many years. How has having it all so close changed you over the long haul. Who looks worse. And who gives a fuck. What you look like. How you fuck. How you don't or can't or shouldn't.

I'm old. And I wouldn't want to be that plug fucking stupid ever again. I don't want to get arrested again.

A32. *I don't mean to obfuscate. I do dearly want to answer your questions. I think I should.*

I have to be careful. But I'm not worried about anything but my own honesty.

I think these girls are especially cute.

Questions 1–13 from pages 72–74 and questions 1–14 from pages 77 and 78 of THE INVISIBLE CHILDREN, Gita Sereny, Alfred A. Knopf, New York, 1985.

1. On average, how many men was she seeing a day?

How many. On average. How many more. On average.
And how incredibly many more behind. How many until it
formed an average. When did the act slide into routine
and the sleazy motherfuckers all tugging their cocks out of
their pants and then leaning back and taking their own
sweet fucking time to cum all clump into the average way
to waste another pay day.

You give these fucks status. Even just by their
singular and collective numbers. By their nick-names, their
number names – first one today, fatass, second fucking
pervert this week, last one of the night, one more and
then I go home – they become larger and more significant
and, mostly, listen, they become better than the little you.
Because you act like you won't let them crawl all over you.
You let them blur into lumps and mist because you let the
decision you don't really care about make you.

And the act that keeps you on the bottom. You
become the vomit bucket used by sick pigs too lazy and
selfish to exert even the effort to make it to the bathroom.
You've been hammered out for just that. And kept clean
only so the next time won't remind anyone of the last
time.

How many can she put away before she breaks
down. How many more can she handle. Until she reaches
that one often repeated but now never equalled act that
she simply must not perform again. Her breathing changes.
Her mind drags. Her jaws clench. Her flesh waxes over and
she fantasizes that fucking fuckable corpse not even one
more fucking cunt fucking time.

You can't get old here can you, sweetie? What
can you do then – toothless, sagged, fatty, fallen – maybe
in Paris, grandma, but not here. Look around. They aren't
here because they've moved on to anything better than
minimum wage and alcoholism and mid-life collapse, lies,
nightmares and homelessness.

The last cocksucker to strip her himself. Let me do
it. It'll cost extra. How much do you have to spend
motherfucker?

I want to fuck the mouth that cries. And I'll pay the extra money and wait all the extra time. Until you figure it out, cunt. My ugly stubby hands on an uglier body used to uglier hands. I want the same technique you give everyone else – I want to see you fall into that careful position that at least takes the pressure off your tired-ass strained back for just a few seconds. If you give a little bit more, a little bit better, a little bit cuter: you get them out just a little bit quicker.

One more hand. To give the other a rest.

Let these animals feel your tit and they'll almost always pinch your nipple.

A finger fuck bigger and harder than a cock fuck because the scumbag's a lot more worried about hurting his precious cock than his dirty fucking finger.

How old were you when you started this? And how do you gauge the perverts when you answer: How you can tell the difference between those pigs that want early teens and those that want so much younger. Oh Honey, I got turned out by my daddy long ago, you know.

And how long before all this new reality wipes over all those lazy lies.

B. DO YOU GET WHAT YOU WANT?

B1. *From today's paper, the Chicago Sun-Times, August 7, 1999:*
MAN GETS 35 YEARS IN ASSAULT OF ADDISON GIRL
An Ohio man was sentenced to 35 years in prison Thursday for abducting and sexually assaulting a 6-year-old Addison girl last year. John B. Ferryman, 25, of Urbana was found guilty of luring the girl into his tractor-trailer with a promise of ice cream last Aug. 23. Police said they found Ferryman that night by using a global positioning device on his truck.

2. Had it always been like that, with all of the pimps, never a day off?

It's easy to lie. I spend 95% of my day in complete

fabrication. Child molesters have to. I can't talk about my tastes or offer small conversational opinions or act immediately on my impulses or in any way imagine that I'm reasonable, or safe, outside my own frightened, burning, perfectly logical head.

It's not about time. I'm not biding my time. I would be watching all that I do now go to waste if that were true. And you can't waste time. It's impossible. You make time livable. It's all anyone does.

B2. *Same paper, same day:*
YOSEMITE MURDER SUSPECT ENTERS PLEA.
Motel handyman Cary Stayner pleaded not guilty today to the murder of Yosemite National Park naturalist Joie Armstrong, who was decapitated. Stayner did not speak during the arraignment in Fresno, Calif. He is also a suspect in the February murders of three tourists at Yosemite. He had been questioned but not held after those killings. The three had been staying at the motel where Stayner worked.

3. What percentage of these seventy or so men a week did she go to a hotel with?

This'll be easy to work out. Then it'll get repetitive too fast.

You don't pay a prostitute to piss in your mouth. How can you give it such a position? And how could you pick apart your own standing on the ladder as lower down the rungs than hers. It's your money, time, need and rationale. Status as what? As compared to others? As compared to what others want and wrest?

She straddles over your face, her filthy sewer filled to flooding with all those other sick john's waste and her own natural proclivity towards disease; smeared and stringing and blocking against all you use to breathe and read and taste and gulp and express and judge. And she expels all the same. In hot meaty chemical wash stink. Women piss so miserly until they become prostitutes. Cheap and unhealthy until it turns to flabby expulsions of vicious imploded hog wash.

38

You prod your fingers into the slack wet nest. And your tongue. And your chin and lips. Your beard, your puffy red cheeks and stinging fluttering shut eyes all becoming meat just like her old pressing female flaps. The center of her dog's life meeting yours. You flatter yourself. You vie for position in blind psycho-sexual advertising. The gutter and the sewer. Pockets and prods. RNA cleaving itself.

Who made your cock that hard? Harder than the last time you remember; harder than ever before just like always, baby. And more desperate now to fuck that particular soaking wet lavatory hole matted with hair and filth and mud and use. That sickening wizening spread open hung human slash.

And then you roll a condom on.

The piss from inside her wracked pin pricked aged body has drenched the back of your neck and your short haircut as it seeped into the rat hotel pillow and down into thick quick dabbing puddles as you raised your nape to furrow more, to gather more human garbage, to sop up more liquor deeper and deeper and swallow whatever little drips you didn't want to miss.

I've seen a cunt drop great yellow globs of mucous and new cum onto an old hotel carpet in the middle of an intolerably hot noon time Chicago summer. While it waited for me to get dressed.

I've fucked a woman who put towels under her ass to collect the possibility of menses and save the college sheets her mother gave her from permanent stains.

I've put my hard cock inside a mother's plug after it's been fucked by five or six or seven of my friends in a row. And watched then as other friends went after me. My next turn would be in her mouth because I learned that I didn't want all that collected boy filth clogging up and washing back on me. The trash was starting to become more and more specific.

I've cummed into pregnant pigs and re-used the holes they abort from. I've fit my fist in them and pissed into their assholes just a little too close to their cunts for the enemas to be especially clean. I've fallen asleep on

them and forced bottle necks inside them and replaced them with muscley assholes quite regularly whenever I couldn't get it out of my mind just how seethingly revolting that pit that these beasts hide and then open for you really is.

And: when I was younger. I fingerfucked them to make them cum. I waited 'til I felt whatever it was deeper in there with my hard-on and waited and worked 'til it cummed. I used my tongue on it. And tried to time my sweating humping orgasm with its.

The same way I fucked young men in crowded movie theatres and had to decide if I wanted their face or their ass. Without barely even seeing either. The same way I fucked old men when I just got tired and sick of faggots and took whatever they preferred. Like a dog. Like a pet. Like a pair of dogs – where one dog is just a bit – what? smarter? alpha? bigger? – than the other for just as long as it takes for one or the other to cum. And then either apologize for not waiting around for the other to finish or just leave silently without even a wink and or a handshake.

When I was younger, a lot more men tried to kiss me. I got offered money. Few wanted anything more than to just suck and lick on my cock and balls until I popped messy or knocked them on their heads and said: It's not working. Thanks but I already came.

I would watch their fat heads bobbing below me and go limp. I would watch them drop and tear and grab and huff and I'd think of something else to help them out.

You don't put your head into a urinal in a public rest room and lick at the drain. And there's cleaner, better kept urinals and there's filthy old rusted leaking pails with old gray pubic hairs and spunk spit and flies and stopped up gummed up plumbing. There's air freshner and nightly clean ups. Old mops in the corner. Abrasives under the sink. Roaches. TB. There's a glory hole porn store in uptown that has a free standing urinal in the back by the locked exit with no door or curtain around it. The queers who zombie around the booths come and watch you piss, staring straight at your cock and your flow, avoiding your eyes completely. Craning their necks around your hand.

40

Letting you know they're focused. They want any dick and this is one way to get it before the other hounds do. It'll follow you as you shake and fasten and head back. They're in the same place as you. And you know which booth to choose. The one that's got another empty one next to it for your new friend. Who's already hard. And who moaned as you turned your illegally exposed dripping cock towards, before you replaced it behind your button fly. Which you didn't bother doing up all the way.

The urinal is female. Like his mouth is. But his squashed face is designed for more, isn't it? Cunts aren't. This is how they're supposed to work. For your deposits. Ask it; it'll tell you. For you to walk up, unzip, and piss your dirt into. Urinals. That are spread open and, if one is a trifle more upmarket, then cleaned and polished after each use. For your disease and garbage and nausea to mar only when absolutely necessary.

He wants a urinal as his face. He wants a cunt. He wants to be the middle urinal in a nightclub where two porcelin johns are full to overflowing with chewed up cigarettes and dried hair and pus and cum and scaly human tissue.

He'll take your piss first and when the stream slows he'll get to give the blow-job he wanted to give anyways. He'll raise his fucking ugly german bald head onto your cock and suck all the nasty little tiresome drops that you usually soak into your underwear. He'll use his tongue like kitchen cleanser and his head like the hand dryer. And he'll slobber and drool out like the end of your cock does after whiskey and beers and faggy vodka and cranberries. Not feeling the end of your bladder. Not feeling the spray on your balls as you make a drunk slobby mess. Not sensing that you may be pissing on the floor or in the urinal or in his mouth and your neighbor's shoes. Just like a cunt. Like a urinal designed for such. Where no one gives a fuck if no one else is watching, especially the runt puerto rican that's employed – barely – to clean up at night.

You release your cum into the cunt.

Into the female face of things.

Into the urinals covered in flesh. In hide. In special little personalities one better, louder, than the next.

B3. *That same day's Chicago Tribune didn't report on the Ferryman case but did carry a photo of a rather bored looking Cary Stayner towering at least a full head over a plump little cop-type:*
YOSEMITE SLAYINGS: Cary Stayner (left), who the FBI said had confessed to killing four women in Yosemite Park, is escorted by a U.S. Marshal after his arraignment in a Fresno court Friday where he pleaded not guilty in the slaying of a naturalist last month.

4. And how long did she spend with each?

She was extra. Extra money. Extra weight. Extra mouth to fill. Extra time to get through all of this.

B4. *Cary's younger brother, if he'd lived, would never have grown to look like Cary. Little brother Steven had been kept and regularly raped by the paedophile who kidnapped him for seven full years starting when he was only seven years old and Cary only eleven. But Steven, after escaping the sex, only went on to die in a motorcycle crash in 1989. Cary says he fantasized about murdering women from the time he was seven.*

5. And what happened after the ten minutes – did she wash?

Where do I find that? That extra. Extra has to find you. That mere unfortunate. A young retarded girl that sits across from her mick bloated pale barroom father in the front seat of his taxi cab. He trots her out at night so he doesn't have to work the at least twelve hours to pay for the cab lease and make enough money to get him and his ugly brood through another day plus liquor.

The mother is a gorilla in a house dress. Fat and tired and comfortable in poverty and noise and, when asked, you can be sure, denies any knowledge of her

daughter's morally revolting situation save her honorable husband's dedicated and unfair work ethic.

The parents should be Hindu. Which would make the mouthing daughter a rat child. Raised to beg and deform. Hairy and bindi-d, the mother would shrill the beast into following her papa into the betterment of the rat's nest forever sat in the middle of an angry hating suburban walk-up. All that white meat pushed up inside all that grease and musty spice; You just shut your fucking mouth. You don't talk about that here.

She was born retarded. And her life here and back home have set in underneath her lumps and bones and twisted the natural warning droops into a hideous urban machine. She has brothers who use her. And she doesn't mind. She responds to the attention and the false devotion and dog pats. And her father is worse. Worse than the mother who needs the money from the whatever-it-is-the-fuck-they-do and the uncles and cousins who don't care to come around much anymore, actually.

Clearly retarded. Far beyond slow. Deep into genetics. An ugly flattened downs syndrome slope into the sunken black ringed bug eyes made all the more tragic by her low end continuous sale. The gropes have to have an effect. The stink and slobber and discharge take a toll. And whatever youthful resilience she might have had were she not so blood muddied and bone soft would even have been worn out and wiped under by now.

That's a lot of dicks the father has pimped.

A lot of excuses and lessons.

That's a lot of use. A lot of wear and tear.

She didn't wash. She wasn't able. Faggots in these peep show back rooms suck as many cocks per day, a week, a lifetime, as she ever would. The hygiene rate and physical efforts had to be the same. You get lucky. Once in a while. The real damage would be in the choice. The lack and need of options. That is, if retards are capable of making groundless lifestyle and survival decisions.

B5. *From PEOPLE, August 9, 1999:*
Cary Stayner's younger brother Steven was kidnapped by a

paedophile in 1972 and subjected to seven years of sexual
and psychological abuse before escaping at the age of 14.

6. Did she look at the man to see if he was clean?

She knows what to do. And doesn't seem to mind. She's
not anxious, however, and leans mute against the rear
door as he undoes his pants and pulls out his prick.

"I had to lean way back and unfasten my pants while she
sat on the opposite end of the car seat staring down at my
crotch. I knew she wasn't going to do it for me. Her back
was all the way against the door – as far from me as she
could get – and I was kinda scared that she was going to
bolt as soon as I got my pants down around my thighs.
Like this might be a sting or something."

She was farthest away from her father at that point. As far
away as she could get when working that night. Her father
offered her services to whoever he thought was drunk
enough or desperate enough or sleazy enough to go for it
without attacking him and calling the cops.
　　　"My daughter thinks you're very handsome."
　　　The father sized up the customer. Just a nighttime
cab passenger until the father eyed them into a john. And
a john that would fuck a questionably aged retarded girl in
the back of a dark parked cab while its father watched.
　　　You want to fuck her: Extra.
　　　You want me to beat off while I watch: Fine.
　　　I would cum right away. Those near enough to
childhood lips on my adult cock and hairy balls stinking like
late night beery pisses and faggot faces chokes deep into
her sputtering pancaked head hell.
　　　I could cum that way. Into her throat and across
her crowded teeth. Better into the condom that I slide
down because she'd only fumble and pinch pathetically.
Her clumsy blather cooking up the equivalent of all those
arabic to irish working rationalizations. Her muddled
impotent rage focused on cardboard boxes filled with
cheap off-brand liquor and soda cans and roach candy in

the back storeroom of the family 7/11 and replaced nightly with the stenched drunken fumes of filthy moneyed gullible sex. This is on the way home, you understand.

She doesn't see kids her own age out this late at night. Instead she sees what she would like to grow up into. She barbies the young women and boyfriends and knows that someday they'll all be her best friends and they'll all share their time and laughs and compliments with her. They would be her friends right now. And very soon she'll have them with her along and they can go sucking the smelly cocks of the dangerous strangers together – and make plans for make-up and TV when their darn typical girl chores are over.

Fifteen minutes: all the way from the bar I work at to home with a quick stop in an alley to unload my disease into this puffy pig's stooped one down, more to go, night.

And her father pretends to protect her. While strangers expose themselves to her. But don't hurt her or make her cry. While they guide her head down to the part they want to mop up clean. And he makes sure she gets paid by taking care of the money for her. Watches as they collapse in her mouth and on the rental seat he'll have to wipe.

He feeds her. Clothes her. Teaches her. Compares the cocks and styles and kinks and slobbings of white drunks and working class bores and has to be prepared for the inevitable guilt and self-hatred that boils up only after they've already cummed. Or, at least, tried.

Most were drunk.

The father could really only solicit very few.

B6. *From TIME, August 9, 1999:*
In the world they try to build, Steven found happiness after his return at age 14 from seven years as the sex slave of a paedophile, and there is no connection between that made-for-TV drama and last week's sequel, in which older brother Cary confessed to four horrific murders in the vicinity of Yosemite National Park.

7. Did she tell them in advance?

Do you like music, sweetheart?

Are you O.K.?

Is there someone I can call for you?

Did you pick this out yourself? It's very pretty.

Nice things make us feel better, don't they.

Looking pretty makes you feel good, doesn't it?

Do you want to go outside and see the city?

It's alright, honey, we'll do whatever you want to do today.

What do you want to do?

B7. *From NEWSWEEK, August 9, 1999:*
Yet he had lived in the shadow of his younger brother: when Stayner was 11, his 7-year-old brother, Steven, was kidnapped by a paedophile and held prisoner for seven years.

8. Did she ever get scared of them?

How do you reach it? How did he teach her? How do you convince it that this is a step upward – this will somehow be better than what she has safe at home. You're not giving in, giving up, sinking lower but, rather, taking a proactive position and struggling, right now only, to change things perfect for the always smiling future. There's a good girl. There's daddy's little girl.

This is what men want and what you do and, try and remember always, this is the proper price and market value.

Showed her porno videos. See the way she moves her mouth and tongue. Look at her hands.

These are breasts.

This is your fanny.

I'll be watching. It'll be O.K. Only do what I say. Watch me. I'll always be there. I'll let you know when something's not right.

I'll let you know.

The girls will like you.

They'll all be your friends. And you can show them what you already know.

Just not yet.

Mom taught her.

Her brothers.

Her sister. Raped previously by her father, brothers, uncle, neighbors.

You force her mousy ratty head down on a fat plastic dildo stuck upright onto a dinner table in the kitchen. Flesh colored and as realistic as the bargain price and suction cup bonus would allow. You bought the dildo at some degenerate porno shop in Chicago on the north side where you drive your overheating back breaking taxi all the fucking time.

You put a twenty dollar bill on the table.

And a can of beer.

A three pack of Prime unlubricated condoms bought from a Walgreens because they're much cheaper there than the exact same brand at the porno joint. The dildo could have been purchased cheaper if you'd shopped during the day at any one of those primpy little fag S/M leather shops that dot the same area as the porno store. But, also, then you couldn't go in the back for a blow-job. And, anyways, you're not looking for professional gear, are you? This'll do fine. The price figures in at the end.

Next to the beer and condoms and dildo stuck up pointing at the ceiling and cash, lies a porno video. Some sale special compilation of blow-jobs and money shots.

Show her first.

You put your mouth here.

And you go down.

Your hand goes here.

And you squeeze and pull.

You can lick here if it's taking a long time.

Do you know what I'm talking about? Do you know what you're looking for – what we're waiting for?

If they don't want to put a condom on; you have to know how to do it yourself.

Here's how you open it. They open extremely easy. Don't use your teeth. Try not to show them your teeth. Try not to be so friendly. Try and remember what you look like when you're doing this.

You have to be careful to get the right side to furl down. Be careful here and pay attention. If you go too fast and just plop it down and then realize you've got the tip upside down – then you'll have pre-cum or maybe germs on the end that you place in your mouth after you fix it.

This is how you roll it down.

Look for warts and bumps and scrapes on the balls. Lick there if it looks clean. Otherwise, don't worry. But hurry up – don't take so fucking long. You'll see how much licking down there helps speed it up.

You'll be able to tell how much the man likes it. He'll tell you. He'll show you. Normally, he'll moan and arch and help you to do the things he likes best over and over again.

Here's what it tastes like. Put the condom in your mouth.

Don't ever make a face. I don't care how bad it smells. Remember to hurry up and get it over with and not bother the man. If you do it right it'll all be over very quickly.

Here's what you do with your hand again.

Suck in harder.

Pump your fist and your mouth at the same time.

He probably won't feel your tongue through the condom, so go back to the balls.

Don't get scared if he touches you. Don't worry. I'll be there to help you if I see you need it.

Take off your top.

Show him your breasts if he's taking longer than he should.

If he says he wants to see your tits – that's what he wants – to see your breasts. Look at me – I'll let you know if it's O.K. – wait 'til I say do it.

Let me see your tits.

Shake them at me. Like you'd do if you had any. Like you could do if you weren't so young. And stupid. Fat doesn't count.

Lick the air like you've got a cock in your mouth. Like a snake. Go on. Like you've seen on TV.

Grab your chest. Those fucking retard tits.

Pinch your nipples.

Do it. Keep doing it until I say stop it. You fucking – you fucking retard. Keep doing it. Grab them. Act like you want to finish this for fuck's sake. Move.

How come you didn't take the twenty bucks and give it to me like I told you to?

Give me that money.

That's a seriously fucking stupid mistake.

You have to be a lot more careful.

You have to think, you understand?

Finish this fucking thing. Finish the job.

Put your mouth back.

Suck down lower. Fit it all in your mouth. Deeper. Go down. Don't choke. Don't be so fucking stupid. Don't make noises. Just keep going. Jesus.

Use your fucking hand.

And your tongue.

I can't keep telling you.

Move your ass.

They'll grab your tits like this. They'll feel your fat ass. You can wiggle. Do you like that? Is that better? Fucking better ...better fucking do it. Just go deeper. Go all the way down.

Rub your teenie tits up against it like that.

Wipe your nose.

Move your fucking fat ass and bend your back, idiot. Rub your tits on it like you wanted to – like you want to rub them there.

You can't see with your eyes closed.

Clean up your mouth. Wipe your fucking chin. Pull your hair back.

Keep using your fist. Use both hands. Suck it harder. Pump it up and down, squeeze harder, make him cum in your ugly fucking sloppy mouth. That fucking hole I have to keep looking at. Move your fucking neck. You – you simply can't be this fucking stupid. This fucking female.

Let me show you the video.

I'll show you what you're doing wrong.

And why you're doing anything at all.

What's the most important thing here?

Did you remember to give me the money?

I'll have to take it from them, won't I? I'll have to make sure your stupid ass gets paid for working. I'll have to do it your whole fucking life.

I'll have to because you'll forget.

B8. *Steven would have looked different as he got older. Carried the marks and knowledge of rape and sexual abuse. In the way you'd have to be careful around him and the way he stared at the things he may have wanted to fuck. The way he held things and the way he used his hot breath. The way these young adults who hang around the peep show backrooms mutate after just a few months of easy access and cheap satisfaction. Their jowls, their chins and lower lips. Their eyes. Their features shape around the mannerisms they've learned to shark and feed. They mold around the act and slowly become unrecognizable from the photos that their broken-home parents keep of when all children look like they might grow up into the same proud gene pool.*

9. Did she ever say no to anybody?

The beer'll take the taste away. It'll be a treat. And it makes it easier to move on. Just a few sips 'til you understand what to do again and again and again and then you can do it easier. The liquor will taste better. It'll make you stop thinking about the head count if nothing else.

I can't keep it cold in the cab.

Don't get sick. You'll see. It'll all be fine and only you can make it seem bad. No one else thinks it's bad.

The beer will wash all the rubber taste and flesh and hair and dirty stink away down your throat and into your big belly.

You don't have to be scared.

You'll barely be there.

What do retards follow exactly? Thought to thought?

B9. *Mike Echols wrote a book on Steven Stayner's case. He later went on to write a book about a priest that molested even more boys than the "reverend" that so enjoyed Steven. Mr. Echols now commands a website that aggressively promotes the brutality and horror of child molestation which, of course, is one of the better sources in terms of disseminating the photos and details paedophiles so quietly, desperately want.*

10. How can she tell?

Men get righteous after they cum. They feel filthy and ashamed. They feel guilty.

It's no reflection on you.

B10. *Rita Ackerman's paintings center around little girls in little tight panties and tiny tops. Playing with naturist animals often enough and sometimes splattered with painter's red to look like menstruation or rape or both seeing as art allows the perfectly noncommittal. The girls are done cute cartoon style. Like the ones girls would draw when they're young even up to the eighth grade fantasizing about what it is to be a girl now. And like the ones older girls draw when they've become disturbed by great fearsome waves of violence that can't nurture and appreciate – honor and celebrate – the true essence of idyllic gentleness and communal giving. The soft touch forever scarred and calloused over. And like the ones boys would draw on paper in school notebooks when they're horny for girls they haven't touched yet. Ones that they don't understand. These boys would become paedophiles as they grow older. Longing for those feelings that seemed to translate somehow magically as their boiling brains transformed lust into fingers that marked and scratched panties and curved the slight hips and lips and titless chests. Most boys would eek out cartoons of big mouths and crude jugs and fat long cocks invading fatter holes. But those with the right or wrong tendencies could appreciate the younger girls for what they should be rather than what they could be.*

11. But what about physical things: would she say yes to any man, even if he was physically repulsive to her?

He plays the video at her and, before she can grow bored, and before he explodes, he pulls his shorts down and waves his runted sweaty irish dick at her. He massages it raw and red and pug'd and greases his narrow stare at her tits. Puts his mouth to her. On her deformed body parts that he chooses one after another. Lips like a father would kiss. Mouth and tongue like a father would lust. Nipples through her shirt before it seeps through how deeply ugly she and this act are. How low he'd have to bend down to find that comedy cunt. Her legs in the air. Her eyes towards the ceiling and then back at him, waiting, learning, staring, not making anything happen for him but warm hated mannequin. Like a cow. Like a warm cow's body. The guts inside like anyone's and the udders and horns and spots and hide just exactly like hers.

Suck it like I showed you.

Make the cum come out. Like in the video. You're as pretty as her. You're exactly as pretty as her. She has more make-up on. You'll look like that. I promise.

You don't need a condom with your father. I'm what made you.

This made you.

Get used to that. That belly, the thighs, the black stench of his asshole and sweaty male crinkled hair. The girth. The sucked out muscles and fallen thick folded sac and crawling veins. His daddy fingers and sleepy dumbed drool, dead eyes and hung mouth.

It's a retard. It was made this way. With a face pulled and stretched out from his wife's. He checks the resemblance underneath the new damage and fresh changes. Every minute. Every single day of its life under god given twists and divots. How do you measure round?

The slanted way she performs everything. Pet tricks for pet snacks for dad, the first time only, and everyone else in the back of a cab at night in the dark parts of Chicago alleys.

B11. *I used to wait at the window of the third floor attic in my parents' house back when I was, I don't know, maybe fifteen or sixteen. The attic window faced the public grammar school I used to go to.*

I would kneel on the floor with my body as much to the side of the window as I could hide and then masturbate as I stared at the little children playing during gym class and recess. I would often pretend to be sick so I could stay home from high school if I thought it was going to be a nice day outside and the teachers would let the kids out.

12. What did she do when she got back to the hotel after work?

She'll never grow old. Not in the way you're supposed – expected – to.

"My brother was a cab driver and he used to get hit on all the time. All these guys late at night would ask him if he'd like a blow-job or if he wanted to come up to the apartment he had just stopped in front of. They'd ask right out if he was gay or lonely or wanted a different kind of tip or if he'd like to make extra money."

B12. *I didn't want to see the kids who were close to my age. I wanted to see the littler girls. The ones in bright clean pastel shorts and t-shirts without the faintest hint of eighth or seventh grade buddings and pretensions. All they should do was run and jump and scream and I was spoiled for choice to find the one I could concentrate extra hard on. I wanted to pick one and stare it down into the ground as I worked on myself. Just chewing on every little nuance and skinny set of legs and white socks and mother purchased shoes.*

13. When did she eat?

The husband stands in front of the wife, wanting to tell her everything.

Instead he lowers his head and starts foreplay. He licks and waits and sucks and kisses. His hands stroke and pet and push and hold and steady and finger as gently as he can.

He wants to tell her about the cab driver he wanted to suck off. The cock he needed at that moment when he felt it was alright to give in to himself. How he thought about it for years and years.

He wants to warn her about the possibility of hepatitis and syphilis and, just now, figures he loves her somehow enough to not want to hurt her or their children or their completely necessary trust.

And he sees the way she acts when she cums. The way he does it to her. How she allows herself to feel that safe and selfish and the deceitful gratefulness that's going to bubble over next.

He deserves better.

He deserves what he wants.

She can't possibly believe this shit life that screams so obviously empty right now. Like old dogs that know better than to go back to the hand holding the rolled tight newspaper, still unable to run anywhere else. Right back up to it again. This fidelity. This respect. This wedge in your life that splits love to one side and sex to the other.

B. DO YOU KNOW WHAT YOU WANT?

B13. *The boys were alright with me. But the little girls were all 5-year-old Sharon Steward.*

From my teenage window, I once got a chance to watch two little boys fighting. They were probably the same age but one was much taller than the other. They fought like little boys do when they're that age – five or six or so – going at it like crying little rages. Flailing their bony arms and stretching their fat heads as far away from the other as possible, while they extend their claws and legs right back at their best friends.

The littlest one got conked in the head when the older one pushed him down onto the hard short grass and dirt. And I remember wishing so fiercely that they should

have been fighting on the concrete stairs that separated
the grass and dogshit on one side and the huge gravel
play area on the other.

**1.Did she think, that it was time to stop? She looked
ill – would she come to a doctor with me?**

The fat lazy slouched mick hardly implodes. The problem is
with the law and then with the miserable bastards who
can't see sex as anything but filthy dirty cunts and disease
and drug addiction. The body fearing puritans. The lonely
moralists riddled with hang-ups that can't even scratch
their way to his meager mastering of contemporary
capitalism and sensual utilitarianism.

Maybe she'll cum.

And it's so much less personal exploitation than a
job at McDonalds or even IBM and these corrupt pre-set
minimum wage boosts.

He's no fucking sand-nigger with his fucking
tandoori fingers all over his rat brown daughter's clay oven
heating ass bitching about the crippled situation back at
home and the sick stingy greedy motherfuckers over here
who strangle the entire fucking world.

Maybe she'd make these simple empowering
choices for herself if she could think past kindergarten.
God, after all, gave her those fatty thighs and meaty cunt
and tits and then kicked the supposedly sleazy black
thoughts in the little minds of all those men and boys who
see the body first and personality only after they've
weighed the rape factor.

She learns like strippers learn. She learns like
secretaries and CEO's have to learn. It'll just take a little
longer and some extra work on the visual obstacles and
people's deep Playboy doll prejudices.

B14. *I wanted to see the small boy bleed. He was crying
and it excited me tremendously. It was one of my best
cums – in the vulgate – and I remember it vividly, even
today. For years afterward I would refer to that little red
faced rat bellowing and entreating and angry whenever I*

thought that maybe I had a chance to drop a quick load
and found myself without a visual aid. It also, I'm sure,
reminded me of Sharon.

2. Did Cal know she was ill?

You use a condom to protect yourself. The men carry
diseases and viruses in their bodies and you don't want
any of it passed to you. The answer would scare her. You
don't want any slow boiling excuses in her head.

"The father handed her the condom. While we were in the
back seat. Like he was giving her change. I gave him the
money and while I was doing that, she had come around
to the back. And she just sat by the door while both me
and the father kind of waited for her. So I finally figured I
better get started."

"Like I said, she watched me unzip and I even had to wave
my dick at her a little. To sort of get it hard and – you
know – to let her know to come on."

"The father watched but not like a creep or anything. Like
a cashier or a bouncer. Which is what he was."

"I had to put the rubber on while both of these scumbags
watched me do it. That didn't exactly get me going, you
know. And while she was sucking on it, I knew that good
old flanagan was staring at me and I watched him back. I
was trying to get in to it. Into her fucking head and
everything. I tried to feel that fucked up monkey mouth on
my cock but it's near impossible with the condom on. She
was alright though. But she wasn't making much noise
which meant she wasn't even sucking that hard and I
could barely tell if I was having sex or whatever.
     And the father could tell. So he says something – I
didn't hear it exactly, I don't remember what it was – but
she heard it right away. 'Cause I'm sure she's heard it all
before and just the initial bark of his voice probably lets
her know what to do. Like a dog getting orders and

responding to tones and timing.

So she flops off my limping dick and yanks the rubber off, balls it up in one hand and with the other starts to beat me off. Tight. Then, before I can say I didn't pay for a fuckin' hand-job, she hunches back down on it. Lots of tongue and she gets it all wet on my piss-hole and she starts sucking my balls into her mouth and then pulling at them with the one hand that doesn't still hold the rubber. I don't think she wanted to litter the back of her dad's cab."

"I came in her mouth and she didn't pull off until I popped a few spurts. Like she was afraid I'd stop mid-cum and get angry or something. I already paid. So she let me cum into her mouth and the idiot must've swallowed some of it because she didn't hock it out like some more professional crack head would have."

B15. *The girls in the playlot were Sharon in clothes. Waiting to be stripped and locked in the closet. Waiting to be released from the scary deep dark and then photographed naked by adults with fingers pointing and hiding and pressing and helping and soothing. Waiting to be hurt. Waiting to be kept crying.*

3. Was it still "kinda fun" on Eleventh Avenue – blow jobs in commuters' cars, hours of standing on freezing corners, hidden moments of refuge in diners? Continual fear and now continual pain? Was that really better, as she had also said when we began to talk, than an office job?

"I immediately started to worry about what she gave me."

B16. *I was masturbating. I was forcing the context. I was responding to the information and regurgitating it through my body.*

And I'd clean up. And worry that I might be seen and caught. I'd clean up very carefully.

4. But she wasn't making any money, was she?

A photo of 9-year-old Amber Hagerman reveals a smile suspiciously similar to that of 7-year-old Meagan Kanka. Amber had dark long bangs hanging right down to her eye brows, shading and almost blocking her little puppy eyes. And these big teeth. Jagged and crowded into a very workable mouth. She doesn't seem as chubby as Meagan but her nose and the size of her eyes all too closely echo the younger blonde's.

There are so many women artists who sell the subjects so dear to a paedophile's raging constant tastes. The painters featured in a lavishly illustrated article by Hannah J. Feldman, "The Lolita Complex" in World Art (#2/1996) are said to be producing work that <u>directly addresses the pre-adolescent and teenage girl in constructions of female desirability.</u>

And.

<u>Today, Lolita provides women with a transgressive model for representing female sexuality: To be Lolita means to take control of one's power over men, and to reverse the pejorative connotations of aggressive sexual behavior.</u>

But.

<u>Could it be that the energy society puts into curtailing childhood sexuality actually affirms its desirability, precisely by keeping it illicit? If so, then the new celebrations of Lolita ultimately reinforce the stability of this desire, playing right into the hands of those who want it, and often to destructive ends.</u>

Amber's mother hands out the posters with the photo of her missing daughter. She chose the photo. Remembered it and went and found it for the printers.

Meagan Kanka's mother sits in the courtroom where the man who raped and murdered her child argues against the loud violent sexually explicit details.

One of the few white cab drivers in Chicago goes prowling through the taxi parking lot looking for a license he can steal and post over his own while he drives on the nights when he brings his little daughter and her drooping wet lolita mouth with him. Sahib, Abdul, whatever works

for however little time he needs. There can't be that many takers. No one will think twice if there's someone else's ethnicity over his own. The little holes don't have to worry too much, if she worries at all.

I thought of offering to buy her panties.

He should carry a camera with him. Blackmail, child pornography, performance art. More money. More violence. More protection. Clearer memories. Proof.

He doesn't want to do this, of course. You think he likes this kind of life? Dealing with scumbags like you – even if it's just for a fucking ride back to your air-conditioned knick-knack TV hovel.

Don't think I haven't stopped in the middle of doing whatever it is I do and grabbed my saved xerox page of Amber's missing poster and stuffed it down my pants. Ripping it and smearing it and taking it back out in crumbled pieces and cuts and, when I was done, laid it on the floor and tried to put it back together again. Not to keep it. Or moan about the loss. Not to torture myself over something so silly and removed that's nonetheless been transformed into an incredibly precious icon. Absolutely not. So I can spit on it. And finish myself off a second time. Right in a row. This time, over myself. This time, over exactly how desperate the damage is. The hoarding. The hunting. The mother and her fucking fucked kid's photo and my cock, my thoughts, all over her and it. And it. All over it and I'll wipe it up – my cum on a wood floor where I splotched over the torn pieces of her little fat white trash face and the miserable cloying words chosen for effect and pity and manufacture and repeat and gossip. And I wipe up the small puddles of infection and filth with the paper clumps and wad it all up and flush it down the toilet. Still excited. Still not spent. That's twice now. And it's only me and my hand and the pictures that were placed in my fucking fat lap. But I'm getting older now and I physically am unable to cum quite that much again and again. It doesn't happen so often these days. Less and less, as I get older.

B17. *In a catalog, a little salesmanship next to the printed*

synopsis on the front cover:
6 X 9. cloth with DJ. xiii + 236 pages. With index,
bibliography, glossary, and reproductions of the interdicted
material! $45.

**5. But if she got herself into a position of holding a
job, any ordinary job, the money she earned would be
hers, wouldn't it?**

From the only monograph I could find on Marie José Burki,
eponymous, published by Camden Arts Centre, London,
and the Bonner Kunstverein, Bonn, in a chapter titled
STRAIT OF FABLES, written by Alain Cueff (page 28):
    The women of Antwerp filmed by Marie José Burki
are prey to an ordinary fatalism, selling a body that no
longer belongs to them, that they have learnt not to
consider as their own, and that unenthusiastically abides by
the law of supply and demand. Standardised by the
elementary conventions of seduction, wasp-waisted and
bug-bright, in a few basic gestures they absently mime the
call of a desire deprived of identity: and when a man
comes, he is not another but always the same client about
whom they already know everything, both his disquiet and
the indigent limits of his want. For the woman of the
streets, waiting is part of the job.

B18. *The key point from the front cover of THE SEX
OFFENDER AND THE CRIMINAL JUSTICE SYSTEM by Ronald
M. Holmes, Ed. D.:*
The differences between transvestism, transsexualism, and
homosexuality are explained, and several chapters are
devoted to crimes against children, including paedophilia,
incest, and child pornography.

**6. But what was the difference *what* the amount was,
if it wasn't hers?**

How many beers does it take to get a retard drunk?
    Give her another beer.

B19. *Another from the same catalog, reproducing the text from the inside flap of the dust jacket:*
In THE LOLITA COMPLEX Russell Trainer investigates the intimacies of real-life Lolitas and Humberts, using case histories, professional opinions, court transcripts, interviews, and police records. The book provides an abundance of case studies of such relationships in different parts of the country. These real life dramas demonstrate the prevalence of sexual experiences between young girls and older men, and the reasons for such relationships are carefully analyzed.

7. Isn't it extraordinary, to do what you're doing for free?

How do you know she was retarded?
        Give her another beer.

B20. *I would see their bodies through their clothes. And I really didn't care. Except for what it meant for them. I saw that little mop called Sharon featureless and crying. Features meaning personalities built from lumps and the lack of lumps and promise and mistakes and misfortunes and blessings.*
        Her face contorted and squeaking silently in black and white, you know. These children were all over the place.

8. Well, did she like it? And did she think the other young girls did it because they enjoyed it?

It was his dick. The one she sucked. You and her. You both sucked his cock. Sahib's fatty greasy nigger donkey dick. His third world cum. His idea. His choice. His eye. Your cash for only a few hours before you gave it to him. His daughter. Your doggie dick. His mouth. His bad genes working perfectly well, actually.
        What about the possibility that someone, other than you, would have been offended by the offer. Outraged by the depraved and brutal humanity as well as

the smeary personal insult. So incensed over his predicament that he beats the lazy irish white trash cocksucker near to death with a crowbar found there in the backseat of the cab. And thus rescues the little beast screaming to a better life away from the filth and hands and body lard into a full home for quieted drugged up grazing knitting cows.

You didn't think to help her.

At least to offer her a place to stay while the police booked her father and you could fuck her in the comfort of your own clean bed. Sink your red stretched cock into the entire teenage abrupted mess again over again and work to convince it that this was better – and different and special – because it's love. And this sort of fucking and mauling and probing and fingerfucking comes along with respect and equal portions and overarching concern.

Do you understand, sweetheart?

Are you happier, dear?

There are mothers for this sort of thing. Outside this cab and away from her leeching father and you and your mad money. Away from the reporters and trivial lessons and great numbers of this shit everyday. In every city. In every cab.

What were you going to do anyway? At least she thought dad cared. Which means he did. She didn't look beaten and depressed, just retarded and listening.

B21. *Their mouths would open wide. As wide as they could. Even from as far away as I was I could see their bulging tongues and tiny teeth and red cheeks.*

The haircuts that adults would pick for them until they were old enough to pick them for themselves. This is best for her face. This will be darling. What do you think of this one, sweetheart?

9. Yes, she knew it was a flea-hole, but it was better than being out in the street, wasn't it?

Did she have a quota?

Based on money or customers?

Did he make excuses for a bad night so that she didn't feel it was her fault?

Is there a possibility that this was a one time complete rock bottom breakdown. A father turns to the only and worst thing he can when his gambling bill spirals out of control. After watching his slow daughter sucking the cock of a stranger to help him in such a small pathetic attempt to make even the smallest incremental dent in his debt, the father epiphanies how bleak the world and his own character really are. He only tried to consider the retrogressed outcome: She'd be even worse off without him here to take care of her everyday.

B22. *They didn't seem especially fragile. In fact, not fragile enough. They didn't cry enough. They shrieked in loud children worlds and stupidity.*

10. What did she think was most important about herself as a person: That she was a female? That she was pretty? That she was young, and bright?

Did she know how to dial 911? And what to say so that the cops could help but not cause such a monstrous scandal. Just say we were attacked and robbed. Don't tell them what we were doing – what you were doing.

Did dad work these possibilities out before hand?

B23. *Like nigger children on the L-trains. The mothers won't shut them up. They peal at the top of their strong little lungs as much as they can before crack is allowed to wheeze it all out of them. But for now, they are encouraged to scream as much as possible due to a deadly combination of utter inaction and boredom on the part of their minders and of their ignorance towards their embarrassing futures.*

And the idea is to hurt them way beyond their stopping. To keep hitting them again and again until they replace the initial shock and ache with more fitful frantic bouts of anger and rage and fear that this pain will never

stop.

You hold their arms back behind their backs and yank up, bending the skinny little brown limbs to breaking. And you slap them repeatedly. On their fatty cheeks again and again until welts that the body creates to cushion the pain coming fast start to rise and push through caucasian. You twist their wrists and pull their arms back up higher. Let them know they'll never break free. And keep hard palm slapping through the screams and sad vengeful desperate attempts to bite at the adult hand that sears and stings.

11. What did she think of herself?

She watches her father masturbating in front of the TV night after night. She takes in all that she can and doesn't imagine herself or him in any way depleted. He'd watch regular TV channels and after awhile could no longer hide the aggressive excitement building up over all the women in bikinis and lolitas and sex rape newscasts.

She's retarded. It didn't start out fair. She doesn't know it should somehow be bad. And it fucking isn't. It's natural and ubiquitous. It's fucking network TV.

His fucking sex drive has fucking increased since he's gotten older.

B24. *It does become rape. A cock doesn't need to penetrate. But it always does, doesn't it? It seems more selfish – more personally honest – with the sexual element washed all over down upon their tiny sexy bodies.*

12. But looking at it another way, it was the pimps who were telling her to bring $150 or whatever every night and she had to do it. If she didn't then they "kicked her ass", wasn't that right?

A finger is all that would fit in at first. He could break her in and lessen her pain just at least that much. He could break her in by letting her brothers in on her. Let them see her when she was dressing and undressing. Your sister's

going to be needing a bra soon, don't you think? Closer in age and better in size.

B. DO YOU GET WHAT YOU WANT?

B25. *I'm not rich. I'm no longer young. I've become what I've surrounded myself with. Which was sort of a surprise, actually. Even though it makes perfect sense. You don't feel yourself sinking – you don't sense the staining and wear and tear. All this depletion. Until the two worlds you've always traversed so easily are both rejecting you and you realize that they have been for quite some time.*

It's not payment. It's not natural. It's not a moral. But I don't think I saw it coming. And I'm not bitching. I don't really know that I don't like it a lot.

13. And would that somebody else be any better? Would he take less from her, give her more – not just in money, but in feelings? Would any of them be honest?

The brother wasn't retarded. Wasn't particularly raised to be smart either. And didn't mind in any case.

Most half drunk customers aren't going to even think of being interested in her slovenly cunt and the time and trouble it would take to spear something this young, this gone, this sold.

She's not like other girls at that age. Not fragile, not confused. She's been served up way too many times. You don't want a dowdy old milk mare just because it's still the youngest in the stable. Especially if it's blind. In any way.

It's putting her approximation of all those other girls her age on the end of your dick. This makes me look good, right? I want a nice hat like the girl next door wears. Why can't I go out and play with them. Hello! Hi! What's your name?

She's already said goodbye to her chances over choices. As she got older than just born. And again, meaner, when her father bundled her into his cab to go

play bye-bye in the car.

B26. *You should see the sweat that rolls off of me. How I carry my weight and age and demands. You should see me in my element. And you should see the others.*
There's a fucking big difference. But I don't know if you'd be able to tell.

14. A game at which the pimps are clever. But what about you? What are you getting out of it?

"It's stupid suffering over some unanswerable hatred for the drives in your body. It's fucking ridiculous. I don't have to explain what I did, or want to do, to anybody else but myself. Your body forms scabs over cuts. It takes perfect care of itself."

C. DO YOU HAVE ANY REGRETS?

C1. *I watched it happen. I always watched what happened. I know what a voyeur is and I don't believe they really exist.*

Questions 1–25 from pages 218 and 219 of
CONTRARY TO LOVE, Patrick Carnes, Ph.D., Hazelden,
Minnesota, 1989.

1. Were you sexually abused as a child or adolescent?

You make it look like a cunt. You decide. You create the atmosphere for such idiotic excuses: The ones they give you to make themselves look all better than the stupid cum rags in their mirrors. Don't make it your fault.

Prove it. To them. Try this: Get up and move to another seat. While the stripper in front of you dances and jiggles and waits to be rewarded in all things currency, respect, safety and admiration. Get up and walk to another.

If the stripper has fat deposits between her knees and ass. If her tits are too small, her nipples uneven and if you see immediately that she should know better than to take her clothes off. That she shouldn't be allowed to get away with it.

Her tit job is sloppy and too obviously fake. Natural is ugly and her attempts at denying have fucked up. Even worse. She should not have settled and your mum acquiescence will not make it any more acceptable. Get up and leave her dancing to the dirty walls and moron bouncers.

Stretch marks. Bruises. Bad dancing. A high forehead and dumbed eyes that beseech her audience for cash over taste. A gap in her teeth. A fat nose. An overly ethnic countenance. Blue new age girly tattoos that'll just look worse and worse as she ages disgracefully.

Hips that are secretaried fat from years away from dancing and minutes away from feminist.

A scar on her face that looks suspiciously like a corrected hairlip. Bad make-up over pock marks, acne or cavewoman eye brows.

If she has a book of poetry privately published. A zine. If she is an underground filmmaker. If she considers herself something of a journalist because she applies college theories to easy interview transgressives. If she has a comic book. If she doesn't know how to dance for men.

C2. *Sex seems so brutally unnecessary and unimportant after it's spilled into your daily social existence. It's why*

AIDS is so unlike any other disease. It's why financial ruin and arrests and jail for sex crimes seem so much more horrid and draconian. Why Leeza and Oprah audiences get so angry. There's the safe pretence that freedom only exists behind your eyes and the greatest existential tragedy is created when you decide you've had enough of promise over experience. Drive and nature that saddles rather than supports.

2. Have you subscribed or regularly purchased sexually explicit magazines like *Playboy* or *Penthouse*?

This is low priority. That's her name and all her tattoos. It's all of their names. Because here women don't sink. They can try to lift themselves up from a belly crawl. It's on their faces. Strippers who pretend to get away with it. And you don't have to look especially close. You just have to put yourself there to see.

You don't have to forgive. And act like this is OK. Or that they've given of themselves. Something that you want and must be grateful for. Anything you must accept quietly and carefully, non-threateningly, so that they can continue your polite fantasy.

Old. Worn. Used. Hoped. You both know it's not a tip.

A crooked nose with wrinkles everywhere else. Puffy eyes and a smile that reveals jagged pushed forward teeth. She's a fucking pig. To do this. To do this, especially, in that state.

Her lesbian lover who's nothing like a lover and everything like a garbage pail that collects all her dropped personality scabs. How much longer can you do it, honey, we have to get this shit out in the open and deal with it. It's not healthy anymore.

A fucking pancake round face close enough to Downs Syndrome to elicit immediate sympathy and public concern.

All these cunts wear make-up on their faces. And should consider wearing more. Everywhere else.

Mostly, it's those lazy mottled thighs.

It's that stomach pouch. That protruding belly above their cunts that puff out to their dented and saddle-bagged hips.

Old sun skin that never cured correctly from her carefree hippy trash childhood. Loose skin that wobbles on even the skinniest wasted bag of human. Knobby. Wet. Sloppy. Pinched. Folded. Tucked. Moles.

Pretentious faces that wear glasses off stage and dry man fucking long hair that turns and twists into hopeful long tresses rather than thin snapping straw. A meadow smile drooping into a ghetto smirk. They shave the hairs around their gorilla patches that beat up to their navels every once in a while.

Bad genetic mix.

Worse genetic start.

Their children.

Their drink tabs.

Their compassionate hugs and Anne Rice books.

Watch them kiss the other girls' kids. The ones they can't ignore when others are watching. The lines that split between their drawn chubbed cheeks and veins that stretch thick in their necks. The old men they hunch into. Their plans to rearrange the continual grays. Furrowed brows and crows feet. Sunken eyes and K-Mart sales. All their naturalism and inner beauty is neatly adjectived under all their loud cackling arguing stupidity.

It's their asses. And their nipples. And their lips. Their faces and their looks and stares and stoned stalls.

You pay to watch them wait.

Dumb as rocks and asked, amazingly, for their opinions. You simply change your position in front of their mined portion of someone else's stage and look beyond them for another one. A better one.

Could you fucking get out of my way, bag.

When's your daughter coming out?

Maybe some sit-ups?

A different shade of foundation? A new job?

One where I don't have to try and look around your huge ugly fucking face to see your tits and sickly cunt.

Clowns. That pick their faces so they can slather up their new moods. And then deny it.

Star potential.

A new lesson in demeanor.

Speech tricks to rid one of one's slur.

Is there anyone back there who's not quite so canine?

How did you come to think this was going to be OK?

Did you pick out those stockings for the effect you think it'll have on the tourists or the other dancers?

How did you decide on this music? Why did that particular slice of pap resonate with your performance ideas? It makes you look like you care. It makes you look like you're fantasizing. Like you want to let someone in. That you're free for four or so minutes not including the extended dance mix. That you're capable of being admired and reaping the more than financial benefits of the slightest amount of work and ingenuity.

But you don't do anything.

You're just grinding and jogging. You're just wasting time while you're up there. Down there.

You're so obvious. So obviously far from perfect. Which is, no matter how settled you've become in various steps of acceptable, what you really want to believe while you're here in front of all of them.

C3. *I have lots of regrets. But I refuse to see what I've done in the past as having some quiet foaming significant weight on what I've come to do now. I'm perfectly logical. There's a silly little danger in seeing what I've done and what I've thought about in my young years as ominous; as somehow quaintly indicative of what I've been acting out in sublimation all these years hence. Issues. Nightmares. Complexes. Unrequited lusts. I've done the work. I did the planning.*

3. Did your parents have trouble with sexual behavior?

It's not all age. Not right now. It's not all parasitical motherhood or worn out planned obsolescence.

The most attractive thing a woman can do is to say:

"I'm not a piece of junk."

C4. *Apparently, it is assumed that a healthy old age would be constructed of an intrepid will to constantly expand one's horizons. I have actively narrowed mine. My tastes and the way I've chosen to satisfy them would necessarily reduce all other options as I age.*

4. Do you often find yourself preoccupied with sexual thoughts?

I've got my hand tight around my cock trying to get it thicker and harder, quicker, for myself. You understand. I want it to register what I'm thinking physically. And I want to have the girl I'm looking all over look right back at me and see what I'm doing and hiss:

"You don't recognise me?"

C5. *Regret has nothing to do with my tastes. My very careful tastes. And as difficult as the difference between what I view as other people's salient and extreme problems and their ugly similarity to my own social deficiencies may be for you to reconcile, I can assure you, they are not for me. There is a huge difference.*

5. Do you feel that your sexual behavior is not normal?

It often sounds better than just similar.

The *Chicago Sun-Times* for August 12, 1999, written by Gary Wisby, under the headline 1 YEAR FOR TEEN WHO BURNED DOG and next to two photos of ugly thick lipped mug shot'd niggers:

The six-month-old dog belonged to Henigan's younger brother. According to Moore, when the German Shepherd puppy ran away from a pit bull on May 13,

Henigan put it in a trash can and fetched lighter fluid for Thomas, who allegedly doused the animal and set it ablaze.

Henigan's brother, 12, poured water on his puppy and called police. "He was crying 'They burned my dog, they burned my dog,'" said Moore, who listened to the 911 tape in preparing her case. Officers shot the pet to end its misery.

C6. *I yearn for nothing. I see the themes in what I've watched happen and the directions I've looked in and the ways I've grown – twisted and bloated, if you prefer – and I understand that not all that much has stretched all that far from home.*

6. Does your spouse [or significant other(s)] ever worry or complain about your sexual behavior?

You spread your fingers through the run-off. You check to see what's dripped down in here and stayed whole and what's been chewed and transformed into pure forgotten wet waste.

These girls would care about those little defenceless animals. These women would look to themselves and peel apart their age lines and make-up stitches and big red atrophies and fatty cottage cheese pits and pinches and want to examine the exalted princess drowning underneath. The soft pink one clutching the shivering soft lamb and small dumb dog and bored kitty-cat. And they'd know, naturally, instinctively, that they'd have to hide the vulnerable beasts away deep inside their bleeding guts and tattoos and paintings and poems and wads of crunched up floor swept dollar bills so that no one else could ever get their violent little rat teeth into them.

Here a blow-job is not a selfish act. Like the way a faggot would dream of giving one: because he wanted a cock in his mouth. Because he wants to feel the other being pleased and satisfied, impressed and grateful. A sense of worth in serving and performing and teaching and in bowing under a violently degrading truth. They're OK

with it and bolstered by their intelligent deconstruction of gender roles and sensual spiritualism.

"Now there's a dick that deserves to be sucked."

"I exploit myself."

"Is this OK", she asks just before she places the actor's long dick in her mouth. She looks to the camera and spoils the scene. It's that first taste, that first acceptance, that initial recognition and weigh that's most important. And she blew it.

"Just do it, for fuck's sake. We'll take care of the frame."

And the next time she remembers. Watch him unbutton his pants like you can't wait to see his big dick. And when he's entirely exposed and only a little bit still flaccid, don't turn your stupid teenage head back towards the audience to see if you should go ahead and do it now, if everyone's ready or watching, or whatever, and just lower your self into the act like you've been taught by the lessons and lusts and directors and boyfriends.

Lift the shaft up and lick down the underside towards the base. To his balls. Slurp it like you like the taste. Then put the fat head inside your mouth and start to move your head back and forth like he would his hand or you would your ass.

Pretend you're spreading magick all around. Pretend this means more than just your time. Consider the poor exploited unwashed paying a goodly amount to see only one of many multiples of your acting out another's prefab fantasy.

Inside all the distillation drippings slithers a microcosm of hatred and self-abnegation. This sick universe slides around an embryo barely protected from the sensual excuses and metaphysical lies that house all the other dog acts. This is where the money goes.

A faggot on his knees does want to suck on that complete stranger's genitals. And the typical stranger can only see the possibility of sucking off some other's filth as a barter. Like he would eat a date's cunt and wait for a cum or proffer a whore a kleenex. There's nothing to be felt in the act itself. He bends his words and ideas around

the capitalist trades and necessities and sustenance and easily eschews the arrested bullshit need for attention, touch, comfort and inner tickles.

And these animals raising their skirts and fastening double bras around their wide chests to heft their watery fat tits up to their aging necks comply. It's business. But more honest than daily drudgery because it makes comfortable recompense for all those past growing mistakes and sexual abuse and wrong decisions.

And the horny luckless tiny bitches realize: There is no act. Correct. It's not the other sick fuck's bloated and selfish mentality. Absolutely. It's not the hard judgement calls or the brutally unfair uncertain future. Right. It's not their nervousness or their insecurity or their christian bashfulness. Not at all. None of that is what makes life – the time away from one's job – so fucking ugly and so pathetically easy to manipulate and package and suck.

No. What makes everything else ugly and painful comes from the eyes that see it that way. Yes. But.

And the basic truth is that the women who suffer all the searing synaptic anguish this way are, in fact, simply, sadly, ugly.

Their faces. They're ugly.

They're ugly in the graphic sense. Not simply under the perfect ten line or lame in the measuring up done by the evil pervasive media pigging patriarchy.

Simply ugly. Ugly women.

Depleted. No. Deficient. Yes.

And that, no matter what cloak they use to get through the day's needful rationale, will never be acceptable or vaulted.

So the one that looks up and momentarily quells her hatred and rage and instead molds it all into self respect and one last shot, purses her lipstick, steels her eyes, extends her wasp chin and slithers:

"I'm not a piece of junk."

Is lying.

C7. *A child I knew back in grade school had been attacked by another our own age, Maybe nine or ten or so. This boy*

showed me the scars on his back made from where the other boy had stabbed and scratched him with a cheap red hard-point pen.

7. Do you have trouble stopping your sexual behavior when you know it is inappropriate?

Page 135:
He once tried to stick a three-year-old girl in the rectum with a stick.
Page 136:
He once slowly choked a cat to death and another time stuck an ice pick through a dog's head from ear to ear.
Page 143:
Recently he has shown an excessive interest in sex and at age of 12 molested his 6-year-old brother.
Page 230:
Subjects who staged cat fights wanted to see the cats destroy one another.
Page 263:
Examples are pouring kerosene or gasoline on an animal and setting fire to it, tying a dog and cat together at their tails and then hanging the rope over a branch to watch them kill each other, injecting animals with various fluids, and the like.
Page 321:
She begged him not to kill the cats, after he had, she begged him not to leave them there.
Page 342:
Abusers often lie: "My dog got cut on a barbed wire fence."
(Cruelty To Animals And Interpersonal Violence, Randall Lockwood & Frank R. Ascione, Purdue University Press, 1998.)

C8. *I fantasized about doing it deeper and harder. And then turning him around to jab it in his balls and penis and the insides of his little boy thighs. I thought scissors would have been better. It could cut up and mutilate his little dick and stab it straight down into his legs and rip open his flat*

chest and skinny belly and slice up his open screaming crying mouth.

8. Do you ever feel bad about your sexual behavior?

There is no one world. There are little pockets of safety, however, and these little frightened mice can't seem to find them. Hence, it's all their fault. Including the bad ageing.

I guarantee this has happened.

A young black girl tired of her life and her lack of success in raising herself out of the daily dirt of mother earth and urban sprawl decides that RAID Ant And Roach spray may be a finer, quicker, cheaper high than what she's been offered so relentlessly for all these finally fifteen years.

She huffs it straight. Putting her liver teen lips on the thicker spout like she's used to seeing crack heads make do with make-shift bottle pipes, little rose novelty jars and plastic juice containers all stolen from Walgreens. The thin aiming straw had been lost long ago and she leans back to press, shoot and suck in as much of the chemical stench as she can drool.

And I can guarantee this has happened better.

In an abandoned building on the south side of Chicago, hard into the notorious hell of Englewood, an even younger little black grammar school girl had been dragged into a back room off the quiet crumbling dusty street.

Forced to learn how to suck a long bum's nigger hard-on a full year or so before she would have learned on her own.

Had her grammar cunt fucked without the mental images of romance and jealousy and braggadocio that her very first boyfriend would have fed her just a few months from now if she hadn't been so fucking ugly for a nigger girl at that age. How do you get fat in the projects?

Made to turn over and have her tight eating asshole finger prodded first, because he had the time, and then penetrated by the same salty cock she tasted with her

face and womb well before she was able to make the decision to give it up for the right customer for a slightly better sized crack rock.

He made her suck down the very last stinging drops from a battered over rusted can of RAID Ant And Roach spray that he had found in another abandoned building while he drug stoopered and canvassed the area for the perfect fuck and bump hole just before he went hunting for the more perfect fuck and suck hole who just unluckily enough happened to walk right by him where she shouldn't have been walking now, should she.

She gagged on it. The bottom of her throat and thyroid cakked it back up into her acid ripped mouth and nose and burned into her squeezing eyes. Her mouth turned chemical black and was watched, nigger spent and nigger fucked, while it happened. Choking and drowning on toxins and bile and pain created to destroy nagging tiny insects in bigger insect homes.

It couldn't have been worth it.

The rape was bad enough.

And again what was left in the bottom of the certainly empty tin can was drained and banged and shook and hammered down to the last hot drop was punctured out and mange'd into her new bruises and cuts and learned three holes.

C9. *And for girls I wanted to use a long thick knotted wooden cane on. In. To ram it up inside their splayed cunts and bluntly puncture wherever it was that their cunts stopped at and their fused shut hymen wombs started at. I'd beat them until their bruises – flat and dark purple and welling up blood underneath such pretty pale princess skin – split into deep open dark red running wounds. Then I'd fuck those new holes with the splintered and dirty and bloodied wood.*

9. Has your sexual behavior ever created problems for you or your family?

The same aged white girl wouldn't have been so

disposable.

Florida white trash or not.

Wouldn't be around discounted discarded cans of RAID Ant And Roach spray that make it into the hands of rapists plowed on crack.

She wouldn't go skipping across abandoned buildings turned into hide-outs for drug suckers and dog dicked child rapists.

She'd fight harder. Having swallowed the scraping frying bug chemical, her chances of making it to a hospital with her throat puffed out and twisted and her face scarred so deep and red and dirty on such paled peach cuteness would have been better and all the more tragic.

Huge nigger hands all over a little nigger's not ready yet body. His burnt long claw crack fingers finding their natural way into her corpus without a problem or slightest resistance despite the drug haze and low end genetics and crazed pit bull lust.

Little black girls look better when they cry. And when they gag. When she should try to spit all the stomach acids back up and out of her numbed out heated up red raw skinned mouth.

Her parents would find the details, reported the day after her body was found, listed in the local paper full of grammar and spelling mistakes.

And they wouldn't know it.

The girl will have had nothing and received less in the way of help or benefits or chances until a small group of flowers collected from a funeral home and placed in front of the abandoned building where she died has been photographed and passed on to the grieving family.

C10. *And I think that I find that much more sexually exciting now than I did back then.*

10. Have you ever sought help for sexual behavior you did not like?

Her momma finds her stray hair still left in the bathroom sink.

Where she combed out her ratty do for what seemed like forever. Staring at herself in the mirror and pulling and teasing and shaping all that her stingy god would give her and nothing ever more.

She'd contemplate her face there. Her flat wide nose and dark eyes and the combinations. She'd test her looks to see how she looked when she kissed. She'd extend her tongue as far out of her mouth as she could to check out how long it was and if she had anything extra special to offer. And what she'd have to do to serve it up.

Momma grabs a kleenex and cleans around the deep rust stains in the sink. Does she throw away the old dry hairs crumbled in her hand under the tissue or keep such sad memories. Does she store them in a drawer or is she just being silly. Should she cherish this precious angel manna or try and just fucking get over it. Not give into it. Could she even possibly throw them away into the garbage without bawling uncontrollably. Can she possibly change the urge over from utter despair. When she sees her child getting brutally raped and hammered into, her baby's baby fingers digging into the rocks and dirt she can pass by daily. A dilapidated pit that crumbles in the middle of all their continuing lives and remains standing out of sheer old bull-headed promise and well organized planning. The forefathers of this neighborhood didn't count on the incredibly heavy weight of the public's filthy laziness.

My poor baby. My poor baby.

She has to seek help. This nameless faceless mother. She can't deal with this all alone. She can't quit these imaginings from her old yellowed eyes and ears and off her cleaning washing working fingertips and the very constant edges of her smaller brain. The sickness that slipped thick repetitive blobs of useless male sperm and thin streams of rust washed metal stripping toxins bleeding down her daughter's black throat may or may not be only one in a great number of difficult dreams and attempts but she just can't find a polite perspective anymore.

She can't live like this any longer. She should have offered her child more than a dirty smudged mirror in a

peeling and running bathroom when she got home from a dirty hot school every damn day.

Where were the cops? And the doctors who were supposed to save her? And the fucking psychiatrists who could have done some trepanning into that evil dog's motherfucking bursting crack head before he was let out on the streets with his glass dick and his screaming pussy hunting cock. Dogs don't need help. They need to be put down.

C11. *It was never hate. I wanted to put my mouth on it. And my dick inside them. It was sexual and I wanted it even more sexual. I'd bite the boys' cocks off where the scissors wouldn't make a clean cut and then chew it to mulch and spit it back into their dead faces. I'd jam my fingers into the baby girl vaginas and grab the pubic bone to yank it down to my waiting tonguing sucking mouth. All that little girl weight being torn and pulled and pushed and raped again and again.*

11. Have you ever worried about people finding out about your sexual activities?

You don't have enough time.

It's a lesson you learn early.

If I see a child left alone to go to the restroom on his own, like in a restaurant, and that child is just old enough to look like he's proud of going on his own without his father's help or his mother dragging him into the ladies' room with her: I follow.

I've done it quite a few times in my forty years.

And, of course, it only works if the stalls are busy or closed and the little one wants to try and shoot his little works into the urinal. And then there has to be more than one urinal next to each other. And no one else can come in. Or come out of the toilet stall.

It's very difficult to consider, and then find, all the optimum chances.

And then, if everything works out in the architecture and cosmos, then the best you can ask for is

to look down and see the little shit's thin stream of piss eeking out of a tiny squeezed kid dick.

You don't dare offer him help.

Kids are taught to scream these days.

But you've got your own cock out next to him. And maybe you could get it semi-hard in the little time you have and you could feel your adult blood start to thicken and sense the rape that should just rip the little dicked freshness in half.

And you don't dare expose yourself to him.

That could invite the same screams or uncomfortable talk back at the next dining table, followed by an ugly loud scene, handcuffs and bad mother TV interviews.

How close those lips are to your rising stretching erection.

How exposed is his tiny balls and flesh and little cock glans. How simple it would be to reach down and bunch it all up and ask him:

"Wanna know what feels even better?"

But you can't. Not yet. Calm down. Bad move even thinking about it.

C12. *I'd masturbate around that, then, as I do now to photos of smiling little children taken in schools but published in newspapers.*

12. Has anyone been hurt emotionally because of your sexual behavior?

I don't like what's on offer. Pornographers don't like the pornography they make these days. And you can tell. It's all geared down to fake laws and faker taboos and the lazy pretence of having to answer to middle America's dumbed down tastes. There's so little there that's different to the 50's jokes of travelling salesmen, cheating husbands and braved-up twenty-year-olds flaunting their trimmed and thin profligate youth before they return to sensible monogamy and self-respect.

They're tadpoles thrashing around, no matter how

hard, for the most money they can swindle away from the fat old assholes who either don't care enough to figure out what they and their marketplace would really like to see or that are simply too frightened of what those tastes might require in overhead, legal fees and sudden harsh declines in egalitarian mores.

But you can't look to others to give you relief. You have to see beyond relief. You have to leave high school. You don't collect types. You don't fuck bone sloppy mental cases on the wrong end of crack pipes and welfare laws. Homeless cardboard beasts stinking like females that don't wash it off every now and again. Some cute cunt from California, one from Florida, another from the mid-west and an especially drunk one from Paris. One that looks like your sister when you were both younger and that old hooker that was older than your mother even now.

On weekends, back in highschool, me and a few buddies would quite regularly drive down to the slightly worse side of town and buy nigger hooker mouths to warm down our masturbation obsessions. Drunk overcoated naked criminal black oily beasts without the slightest worth save the money we very quickly and politely gave them. Their hotbox mouths only became our fists for a scant few minutes. But their hideous lives and eroding bodies continued to amaze and amuse while we waited for the rest of us to just fucking finish already. It was never quaint. And it isn't now. Not because of the PCP and speed frying out the insides of our judgement. Or because of sentimental adult guilt. Gender and racial parity. Simple hormones. Lazy parents, lazier cops. Stupid teachers, store clerks and pimps.

We'd spend the rest of the long evenings dodging curfew until we could convince our girlfriends to do the same thing the hookers did but cheaper, better and cleaner.

I despised women right from the beginning.

My girlfriend was more than accommodating. Back then, a fuck was easier to squeeze out of your girlfriend's show than a blow-job. But my little piggie, when we were

alone, was rather fond of resting her big blonde head in my lap after we made out because she was, I'm sure, flattered by my anxious and painful erection.

Though that's not why I hated her. Not even because she seemed to like acting like a whore when I unzipped and shoved her make-up into my lap. She must have thought I never bathed. I had to stink so bad. My sticky hot cock and balls and pubic hair had to have steamed up the sick bellows of any drunken cocksucking nigger throat full of stale alcohol, all the earlier greaseball cocks before me and all the cigarettes she inhaled as after sex toothbrushes.

I've never equated my sexual tastes with theirs. Any of them. I don't see how your question could be answered. I always consider my partners' emotions and the chances that they'd be hurt always seemed so fucking silly and immaterial and then, somewhat suddenly, worthwhile.

I never had to tell her that I was cumming less with her because I'd already popped my best load into some busy african slave hole.

Someone else usually would, though, wouldn't they?

That's how my mother found out that I liked little children – or rather, at least, photos of little children. Getting fucked. From the news.

You pay hookers. You go to bathrooms for sex with dying degenerate filthy men. I trade drugs that I get from scum for sex with scum.

C13. *You'd have to think that the ideas were pretty orally specific, I guess. I wasn't going to hurt them anymore after what I had already planned to do to them. They'd most likely be dead like garter snakes nailed to little wooden boards and small dogs smashed over the head with a hammer to keep them from yelping so loudly. I simply wanted their pain to be caused more directly by me.*

13. Are any of your sexual activities against the law?

Last week I got a handjob standing at a urinal in a gay bar

on the far northside of Chicago. There's a slanted mirror on the ceiling over the urinals that lets all the faggots check out the competition and potentials. Some camp utilitarian hold over from more care-free days.

I finished pissing and waited. When I looked up, the skinny queer next to me was staring at my reflection in the mirror, not across at my exposed piss pursed cock. We watched each other's eyes and I stepped back a little to push my cock out a bit further. He snaked his eyes to the real flesh and reached over and squeezed. And started to stroke around my barely guarding fingers into the thickening shaft. I reached back and reciprocated. Suddenly, effortlessly, he had my balls and my cock in both of his hands and his hairy forearms virtually in the urinal. He lowered his face into me and licked the fresh piss slit and dragged his fat tongue down my hard-on into my shovelled out bunched up balls. His head all over the drain because I wasn't moving back any further. I dropped my hand from his soft cock because he was getting entirely too busy. I pushed a bit closer to the running drain. And forced him to retreat to just using his hands. A condom machine was chained to the wall above the pissers and below the mirror and I thought I might be better off encased tight in one and then back into his hungry beating skull.

As it was, I popped all over the urinal. My cum forming a large thick wad on top of the toilet's flushing handle just underneath the condom machine. He kept jerking my cock and shaking the cum drops violently onto the floor, my pants, his tight hand and the plastic trap in the urinal drain.

He didn't ask for anything in return. Sex is most often simple proximity. I patted his back and turned to the sink to wash my hands with the blue goo from the large ostentatious squeeze bottle of industrial strength anti-bacterial soap. He didn't lick the cum off my cock or the flusher. And he didn't wash.

He played the mob-owned fruit machine all night and I sat back at the bar with an old friend and a brand new one who was dying of AIDS.

C14. *From Life And Death by Andrea Dworkin (Virago Press, 1997). Page 22 in the first chapter:* MY LIFE AS A WRITER:

I began messing with men when I was in High School, though, sadly, they began messing with me earlier than that – I was raped at nine, though not legally, since fingers and a hand were used for penetration, not the officially requisite penis. That ended up in my hand as he twisted and contorted with a physical omnipresence that pinned me and manipulated me at the same time.

14. Have you made promises to yourself to quit some aspect of your sexual behavior?

You have to continue to be careful. Sex is also about control. Self-control and age. Youth. Until it becomes age. And with age comes a more steady understanding of what's available and what's best left unsatisfied. And it's the care – the frightened treading in me and, especially, in others that I find so tremendously attractive. Sex-wise.

C15. *From the second chapter:* IN MEMORY OF NICOLE BROWN SIMPSON.
Page 41:

It is always the same. It happens to women as different as Nicole Brown Simpson, Lorena Bobbitt – and me. The perpetrators are men as different as O.J. Simpson, John Wayne Bobbitt, and the former flower-child I am still too afraid to name.
And page 47:
When I was being beaten by a shrewd and dangerous man twenty-five years ago, I was Buried Alive in a silence that was unbreachable and unbearable.

15. Have you made efforts to quit a type of sexual activity and failed?

I work well with the system that exists. The one that allows me to go to a store peopled by trendoid little groupie girls

and rent a porno video that suggests, if not directly mimics, their rape.

I like the idea of holding down any woman and spraying RAID Ant And Roach spray into her tears and replicating what I look for on video into her clutching screaming bleeding raw giving body. Her black body. Fifteen years old. Like Tawana Brawley.

I want to concentrate on hurting her breasts. Stabbing little deep bloody pits into those gross hanging bags of fat with dull bent clean safety pins. Fucking wretched mother pin cushions advertising adolescent pretence to middle aged self-loathing. Cutting them up into slashed ribbons with angled razor blades. Slicing them – its – up and dragging muscle and adipose down in tumorous sized lumps, ripping the baby sucking contorting nipples off with my teeth and blood soaked gingivitis scarred gums.

Blood warm like mamas. You fuck them with what you have around. Dead and choking and fazing in and out having suffered through the worst beating of their toothless lives, you could, I'm sure, jam the entire width of the hard tin RAID Ant And Roach spray can into her cunt, first, easiest, asshole, second, giving in finally and forever hideously distended, and mouth, last, through smashed teeth and torn lips and dislocated jaw and bashed scraped and skinned throat and disfigured closed casket permanent forevers.

C16. *From the third chapter:* LIVING IN TERROR, PAIN: BEING A BATTERED WIFE. *Page 52:*
I was battered when I was married and there are some things I wish people would understand. I thought things had changed but it is clear from the story of Hedda Nussbaum that nothing has.
And page 53:
My breasts were burned with lit cigarettes. My husband beat my legs with a wooden beam so that I couldn't walk.

16. Do you have to hide some of your sexual behavior

from others?

At some point you're going to make a mistake and boil
over into real life, fucking up everything you've ever done
and every chance from then on.

But just imagine if you could get away with it.
It won't be about the cum. Not at all.

You turn away from the urinal and face the little
boy who's trying to hurry up as much as his skinny
vulnerability can manage. Your fag sharing cock ready to
drip piss as much as sperm or syphilis heats up in your
palm as you stretch it out towards the boy's face. And
before you snap back down thicker, your other palm
surrounds the back of his soft haired head and pulls his
frightened face into the slimy overwhelming rape. You
grind your hips like a faggot stripper mimics a younger hag
stripper. Clench your ass and bend at your knees; your
center, your focus in your balls and fattening adult penis.
You mash his screaming life – his eyes, his little pug nose,
his mute sexy small mouth that doesn't know enough to
bite – into your hung sac and stink and full tight wide
erection. And you grind some more. Harder. Yanking him
deeper into it. Feeling his breath and angry hands rising to
your hairy thighs and crumpled hard jeans and bumbling
sloppy all over your sex and his struggling. Harder.
Suffocate. Stink. Fucker. Getting longer and redder and
animal to penetrate and rape and murder.

Put it in your mouth or I'll kill you.
It'll shut him up as well.
Now or I'll kill you and your fucking ugly mother.
Get mad and defenceless when I insult that lonely pig
you're going to leave. The mommy you're not going to
ever see ever again. Put it inside your mouth as far as you
can fit it.

And when he chokes and sputters, you push
harder still. And when he pinches his entire tea cup sized
ten fingers into your meaty thighs and hair and tries to
kick and puke, you push into his open mouthed childhood
even deeper and deeper and blacker 'til it faints clear out.
Its body hardly protecting itself. Which is when you bang

his tiny rat holed head open on the curved and sharp edge of the clean white sink behind him. You grab his little dick as it retreats into itself and lower your face to bite through his minute boy sprouts and fleshless sac. Smash open and crack his crumbling skull again and again on the splintering tile underneath the sink where all the piss stains and stray pubic hairs and shoe shit never get washed up and you get up and run out of the restaurant as quickly as you can. Out the back door. Through the kitchen. And you don't bother with thinking about the keys to your car and the people in the parking lot or the witnesses who saw you go in the back or the people at your table waiting or the neighborhood or the life you lead and the trail you leave.

And you'll remember the little boy's death.

And his tight shrinking balls and the bite and taste of cock and the next time you get sucked off by anyone, male or female, you'll feel his entire six or seven years all over the outside and inside of your pumping slob mess.

C17. *From the fourth chapter:* THE THIRD RAPE. *Page 57:*
I had been raped twice before. No one used the word "rape". The first time I was nine; my parents didn't report it.

And page 59:
I believed then, and I believe now, that still no one had a right to rip up my insides – nor the insides of the many hundreds of mostly black women, mostly prostitutes, in that jail.

17. Have you attempted to stop some parts of your sexual activity?

If you had just exposed yourself to him the ugly outcome may have still been the same. The running part, the hated part, the masturbation afterwards. All that horrible ending for such a quick shot at his eyes and your hard cock. All of that possible in the smallest reduction of a full blown taste, anyways.

How can you stake out the john. How long are you willing to hide and wait.

C18. *From the seventh chapter:* PORTRAIT OF A NEW PURITAN – AND A NEW SLAVER. *Page 68:*

Before I was much over eighteen, I had been sexually assaulted three times. Did I report these reports? – patriarchy's first question, because surely the girl must be lying. When I was nine I told my parents. To protect me, for better or worse, they did not call the police.

18. Have you ever felt degraded by your sexual behavior?

The young boy who watched that cock next to him and became frightened and silent, because of a small natural fear of weakness, only, now finds himself figuring out every possibility and ageing into the same act years and years later.

Just back away from the urinal and aim your piss into the drain. See if the child laughs. See if, on his own, he decides to join you. Backs up his less than four foot body and wants to play too. Two men, he enjoys, playing with how far their pee pee can reach all the way into the toilet. His only fear now that his father will come in and yell at him for making a mess.

His breath so near.

His nakedness so bare and available and unthinking to be stabbed at and snipped sloppy with a pair of sharp scissors conveniently kept in your back pocket.

I'll tell your dad you were being bad.

Never do that again.

And he finds himself forever wanting to replicate that act. Down the slope into size-queening every tea-room and back booth available to suck every single cock he's ever guessed at.

Thank you.

Do you want some head, sir?

C19. *From the tenth chapter:* MASS MURDER IN MONTREAL: THE SEXUAL POLITICS OF KILLING WOMEN. *Page 113:*

Like many women, I have a long history of

violence against me, and I say, to my increasing shame, that everyone who has hurt me is still walking around.

19. Has sex been a way for you to escape your problems?

She's an ugly woman. Twenty something and dressed in catholic plaid – red because, in most cases, green is illegal – and a tight t-shirt and pigtails and a tattoo over her flat navel and the obligatory white knee socks along with nipple pinches and stupid mugging grins.

She shaves her cunt completely.

She's quite skinny.

And when you slice out the bottom of page 32, cutting just below her belly button and the ridiculous flower tattoo you'd be left with a shot highly similar to a close-up of a little girl's childish vagina. Just a slit barely rising between two not too fatty thighs.

The old bitch's pubic area, if you look far too close, looks airbrushed. Perhaps indicating a bad shaving rash or some other bumpy female unpleasantness. But this particular shot – chopped carefully – violently reminds me of the obscene close-ups I've seen scroungy paedophiles focus in on and distribute illegally.

Just down her youthfully long torso and below her boney waist.

And cut before the knees.

No labia, no chewed lips, no maw, no hair, no personality except dead. Just a slight slashed indentation. A curve.

As you masturbate you can feel the give in her pubis. Her tight flat flesh and divot. It's like that. And as fake as the photo and the crop and the giggly danger the cheezy hollywood editor uses as reputation.

You actually don't feel a thing.

C20. *From the eleventh chapter:* TERROR, TORTURE AND RESISTANCE. *Page 117:*

As any woman in this room who has ever been beaten or raped knows, it is one of the most impersonal

experiences you will ever have.
>>> *And page 125:*
>>> We know who the rapists are. We know because they do it to us. He did it to me; he did it to my best friend.

20. When you have sex, do you feel depressed afterwards?

Since I wasn't going to fuck it, the fairly clean looking naked pig slobbed her rubber ass off the towel and onto the sheets. Since I already paid, the fully viewed pig felt compelled to insert almost all of her hand into her fat wet cunt. It had to be wet. Or that fat. Her bunched up fingers sank all the way in far too quick and easy. She was not in the slightest way excited. And I would be surprised if she lubed because I was clear of my intentions not to touch her long before she tugged her saggy girth out of her black sales dress.

I don't know what kind of old fingers she had. Long and withered like her brethren usually hide, I'm sure. I didn't care about her hands except that I didn't want them on any part of me. They should have been soft, actually, she wasn't exactly the thin english type but she was at least as old as thirty and apparently a whore for some time. She shouldn't have had miner's callouses or crack pipe burns. Maybe sewing cuts from the long times she had to sit and wait and while. I'm tempted to guess that's where her lumpy chin and belly came from. Snacks and sitting and smoking. All that talking with the lady that answers the door that takes the make-believe tips. I'm tempted to assume she gets plowed twenty times a day and any kegeling tension she might have retained after her first mistake baby or two had long given way to pure day to day drudgery and coffee naps.

Please don't do that.
Just sit. Please.
Thank you.

She had a sore on her waist. What I think was her waist. It was more on her side horizontal from her folded

92

navel just above her kangaroo pouch of slight unembarrassed after cash cellulite. These British whores are out of their window wear in mere seconds after returning, cash stored next door, to the room you wait in. Just after they called out in the dark that this nice American gentleman has paid you a nice tip darling.

Just don't bite, OK?

The question as to whether or not she's actually had that happen to her just means more noise. Noise under that irritating solicitous accent or, worse, that feminine lilt.

I really am here because I hate this particular beast. And this particular English beast is only as special as the sign inside the wide open doorway off the busy yuppie Soho street.

And, unlike the rest of the dogs and niggers and perfectly respectable quiet businessmen who paw these ragged hideous depths hourly: I pay extra for less.

C21. *Such an incredible charge: The dead dick, or even better, the straining hard-on on a faggot ailing with walking AIDS. Hurting for a touch and comfort and financial security only after his sick tool is emptied first.*

21. Have you felt the need to discontinue a certain form of sexual activity?

What if I only want to look at your tits. When all I really want to do is see your face. On the inside of this room. With the light in the window. That hangs and glows red outside. Model. And the disgustingly vulgar sign downstairs pointing up to here. That maybe masks criminals in the hallway.

And if she's not filth. Not another criminal. Not human garbage used and re-used and drained and spit on and expected to take it and hide it and get ready for the next, maybe cleaner, maybe gentler, pathetic lurching staring scumbag. Then all I really need, I guess, is to pay you here, figure out the exchange rate, and imagine that I've added my very important charitably minded

contribution to keeping you here where it's just a bit safer than the streets. Or, if you prefer, incrementally helping you to get the fuck out of here all that quicker.

I'll be done in a minute.

I'm really quick.

I cum on my hand and on her carpet. On their carpet. This room being shared by whores in shifts. I would have been fine with anything other than what she did: Which was to snake down to the end of the bed and jam her fingers into her womb. And act as if she was giving me extra. A treat for the polite masturbating American at the foot of her rickety server's bed. She moved away while I jagged off and she stared at my gawked face and licked the air farthest away from my cock. She didn't want my cum on her and she could see better from the pillow end. Safer all around. While she dug at herself.

She cleans herself first. She pulls herself off the bed all rolls and tits and finish talk and offers me the paper towel that she placed on the table just before taking her clothes off. One paper towel and an ashtray filled with condoms. The paper towel is considered rude and therefore not in plain view until the john has paid while the condoms are a convenient and leery attempt at romantic advertising. She heads into the little bathroom off to the side and stands comfortably nude at the sink splashing fuck knows what.

I don't want to see it naked.

It refuses to suck its pouch in.

It still teeters in high heels. To hide her corns. To retain just a hint of fetishy safety in the sudden face of sunken worn femalia. A small attempt at weaponry.

It talks. Always. And offers me a chance to wash up next. So your wife won't see the stains. That soak into your skin, underwear and the inside of your crumpled jean crotch.

The hog shakes my hand naked.

Um, about your scab.

Are you in town long.

I'm here most nights. Just look for the sign downstairs.

Rather easy five minutes work, yeah?

Work?

I wouldn't fuck anything I actually like. I don't believe anyone does. Especially after seeing it like this.

C22. *I've seen them. I see them as all the same. But I look hard for the most minute differences. And I get them sicker. Our viruses mutate and create more resilient, more aggressive strains. Metal drug resistance starts with me or with their formal brutal inability to control themselves. And their answers to their tired grieving lovers, bored co-workers, rejected now rejecting family, and their thinning outraged community all include me among their tragic existentialism. Where I absolutely do not belong.*

22. Has your sexual activity interfered with your family life?

I'm allowed to carry on unchecked. I've replaced sex with pornography and realized they're exactly the same act.

The last woman I fucked – actually put my cock in her cunt – was only a few months ago. But I had performed the act so many times before that there was guaranteed nothing new or interesting to be had from inside the pigness of her body. I never fucked her before. In fact, I had never fucked anything that old before. Which is why I actually decided to fuck it, rather than just jerk off or get my condom'd cock licked and mouthed. I've fucked women before and picking out the better parts of what they may have to offer – like crack habits, ghetto children, AIDS, old age, tiny tits, loose financial needs, whatever – tends to still sound too base. I don't hate them. I'm not bored. I'm not primally compelled. But I'm not willing to believe that there's something special in anyone of them. It's my choice. And I keep making it. Like I did a fucking long time before I laid my eyes on anything specific.

This is nothing but pornography.

In Paris, on the Rue St. Denis, I watched all these daylight hookers talk with each other. They stood in individual doorways along the main drag and bunched up

in closer numbers off the side streets. Some wore long coats buttoned up to their necks while others wore tight thin bright sweaters and lacey see-thru tops. A great number sported fake nipples – little plugs stuck in their bras and on their tits to give that always interested, always ready, always young and firm look to their quick ageing wear jobs. All of them wore clown make-up that women for sale carve on: Fat lips to show you where to stick your money and red cheeks to cover the bad childhood and ill health and shaded eyes to convince you to talk right at them about using their bodies fully as urinals and waste baskets.

Do I want a nigger in more make-up than the ones back home bother with. Do I want a nigger that speaks about my money and bad taste in french rather than gorilla. I'd have better luck understanding their fake snotty broken english than the cranked ghetto sludge I usually fuck through.

Do I want a nigger with a mouth.

The black girls are said to be pushing out the white girls. The color ratio has changed rather dramatically since the last time I was here. Picking out a white whore – fat with big tits, skinny with fake – stuffed not implanted – tits, or the newer brand of renegade middle class friend doesn't seem all that much a better prospect.

"Twa Son" or some fucking garbled thing like that slithers out of these cunts' mouths as soon as I approach. They all say the same price to any old asshole who asks in anything other than french. It means 300 francs which, I have to estimate is close to 30 pounds and therefore close to around fifty dollars in this shit fucking exchange rate and, no matter how cheap even on a Thai scale, it's too much for that. Something so perfectly poor.

Pushed further, they'll go down on price. But I'm not interested in haggling. They count with their thumbs first here. And some of these beasts drop it into their palm when I ask for a mite less than the twa son full two holed feast. That gets me washed and sucked sans condom for maybe the first three or four plunges. Then its cunt for more. Ass is another option I'm not all that interested in. It

really doesn't hurt enough. And there's already enough shit in it.

On the furthest end of the street, in the daytime only, sits, literally, all the older hookers. Sixties even.

I'm sure my mother fucks this way.

I want the condom on, dear.

I wouldn't put my cock into my mother's mouth or her cunt without wearing a condom on principle, honey, you understand, especially if she was selling it.

I'm old now. And a creep. This is what I do. I go to where the choices I've made throw themselves back at me. Up and down the middle of this street are porno shops and peep shows. There's a faggot sauna which is rather too expensive and just a bit further is Club 88 which has heterosexual sex shows seen from private booths (20 francs a shot) and, upstairs, very busy, very crowded queering buddy booths.

Mom and I actually had to walk about a block through a tight throng of tourists and tradesmen to get from her perch to her rented apartment. I'm fairly sure she lived here. Because I very carefully only saw one dreary room with a bed and a sink. But it was housed among a much larger hall of many larger apartments. Where everyone else in the building knew what she's done all her life, or after the fall, and isn't it sad in kind of a pitiful sort of way. And, of course, I'm the pig. The gross beast taking advantage. Desperate. And sick. With someone like that.

Keep your clothes on, mother.

Just lift your skirt, mom, and tug down your very necessary panty hose.

Mother's sweater would feel better than the watery mottled hung and sagged flesh underneath.

I promise to be careful. I promise to not put my fingers in or anywhere near the fatted folds between your collapsed veins and thighs.

I initially only wanted to see mom's head on the end of my piss. My dirt. Would look better that way.

I'm not a fan of meat, mom. I am a fan of make-up. And of giving you money. Of confirming your lease. Money is not the fulcrum here. It is the introduction. Sex is

the commerce. The act is traded. The payment is what's sold. Her head. And, now, I see, her wig. Her mirror. Where she watches my hands and pose and encourages me to forget my situation. And the relative dangers and chances and mistakes and steaming rages; hers and mine. So I don't kill her when I see how ugly she is on the wrong end of sex. And how ugly I've become from letting her and her room and her morning make-up struggles and dread infect and stain me.

I pull out of her mouth and pat her head. Her tongue hangs out speaking french dog and I tell her, while I beat my soaked cock up on my own, in her face, that I'd like to put it in her twat. The words help in sending the charges to my balls as does her struggling off her seat on the bed to get ready.

She unbuttons her yellow blouse and tugs her bra up to disfigure her pink nippled grandma dug beyond its natural hang and droop. I masturbate rude. She steps out of her black dropped skirt and kicks it into the corner. Which means hurry up before it gets wrinkled. She spits in her hands out of those pinched red smeared lips and rubs my cock up and down. I do the same. Then she grabs some ointment from a jar on the sink to use as lube and smears it under her belly. I keep masturbating. She motions that I should take my pants off. Again. And I'm forced to. Which means I'll go limp. I'd rather masturbate. But I push my shoes off at the heels and yank my pants all the way off. She's sitting there with a new towel on the bed and an unwrapped condom. That I prefer to put on.

The condom and my AIDS and her old age and stupid fucking concern for whatever little else she may have left makes me fully hard and I sink in. All the way. Silent. The beast all over underneath me.

Such a little girl with such a strong back turns too fucking rapidly into such an old rag with a bent over warped frame.

And I do have to pay to see it.

I pull out and slime the greasy condom off into my palm. The tip giving away and the warm stink of her cunt shit and my fat load wadded up into my palm. So as not

to spill. She tells me in french to drop it into the basket underneath the sink and, before she pulls her clothes back on, hands me a towel. Not a napkin. I toss the garbage away, wipe my hands on the towel and dab my hands into the sink. Struggle to get my pants unbunched. She doesn't say anything else. She gets fixed up and waits for me to leave by myself. I said thank you and she smiled like mothers do when they give you money.

Later on that night, I washed her stink off in the mouth of a heterosexual french man in one of the booths of Club 88. This pig wanted me to cum in his mouth, he asked me to in English, and I told him I didn't think I was ready yet. But I came quickly. As always. The booth was too tight to really form a conversation about why I was in Paris or if he had any children and he didn't seem too interested in jerking himself off or in me reciprocating in any way; so he drained my meager cum and my mother's reused womb and got up and fucked off.

C23. *I've become the fat german tourist in the Thai blow-job bar. The one that the wonderfully young dumb frowning and working hookers look at as their low point.*

23. Have you been sexual with minors?

At this age he doesn't have to make apologies for it. Who would he apologise to, anyways? Himself. Actually.

He stays alive for this. He puts condoms on the cocks he sucks so he doesn't die from this. Not that he would. He falls back on the bench in the one single booth that has one in here and keeps his short windbreaker shut. There are no mistakes here, no misunderstandings. He is here to suck whatever you pull out.

Which he does while he sits. And asks you if you mind wearing a condom: Can I put a condom on?

You'll suck it this way or not at all.

OK, pal, fine, and he taps at your exposed cock meaning: leave.

Do you always use rubbers, this one long dicked hick asked him after returning back to his booth. The

pickings being slimmer than he figured when he barged out so furiously before. The drawn and wasted hillbilly had an even bigger hard-on this time. And yanked it out and beat it up and down right outside in the hallway between the various doors and expensive bored mexican hustlers. Buck thought he had something to show that irritated greaseballs but frenzied the young college students. And everyone was concerned about the law suddenly.

The faggot who runs the place is usually one of two people. A blonde balding lazy queen with too much jewelry on his wrists and fingers and ears, most often found in short jean cut-offs and then a burly dock type who sucks more cock than anyone. This latter mouth is the one I suspect of secretly videotaping most of the booth action. I caught him once masturbating behind the front counter. As if I was his mother, he pulled away from his seat and walked away behind the TV on the shelf next to the register fumbling with his hog gut and too tight pants.

I saw him break up a fight once, just minutes before closing, totally ignoring the complete out faggot screaming: "Call the cops, call the cops right now, I want him arrested". The plug just pushed and pulled out both booth idiots, saying "Shaddup, shaddup, get the fuck outta here before I lock both of ya up myself" shoving them through the front door. Like some barroom bouncer who gets away with enough illegality in his life to not even bother with this little fly and bug noise. I walked behind him. Watching what was happening and wanting to get out of there myself before any cops showed up. It was 2 a.m., I lived about three blocks away but figured it was best to get a cab.

Take out your cock. I'll just jerk off. The hillbilly was back in his booth, having followed him straight in this time. Having picked the one nearest to where the hick was exposing his girth.

The condom was still going to be an issue.

But the trash was hard and horny and fine with cumming by his own hand as long as he had another cock to look at while he did it.

I ain't as big as you, you don't want any of this.

Yeh, yeh, take it out.

He pops his fly and pulls out his meager soft cock and tries desperately to work it out.

That's it. That's it.

The hillbilly knew he'd drop to the floor. That fucking white trash bulk understood everything in the careful cocksucker's head perfectly.

Sex sweated over his wax face like a wet towel being squeezed over his head and the lowering face could do nothing except instinct it all: Started with rubbing buck's balls and then stroking along the cable thick shaft and then simply had to put that fat round apple smooth head into his head.

This is how you get fucked.

This is how you die.

Right now: This is how you receive a viral load that could or could not be the deciding factor in every decision you make for the rest of your life.

He made me.

All that tongue means he wanted it. Fucking slob.

You're not afraid of HIV are you? You can't get it that way. Anyways.

There's a beautiful child down in Florida who got gonorrhoea of the throat from having his father soak his baby mouth in his infected sex sick cock raping sperm.

And you do jerk off later. Thinking or hating.

You like big dicks: the disease asks.

I like your big dick the faggot answers, sinking even deeper into the game.

I like your big dick a lot.

You always use condoms? The certain dishwasher smashes the faggot back home: Standing in the dark closet, reeking like cum and piss and shitty asshole fingers and bad breath and balls and back sweat, the faggot masturbates himself close and gets set to gobble the big dick of his new best friend.

The hick jiggles his heavy balls and inches closer. This is perfect, both facing the porno screen at an angle away from each other. As if they're only slightly embarrassed. Or if the movie might just mean a little more.

The faggot eyes down on the long meat. The hick judges and prowls. Pushing his prize to the size queen deeper inside every single queer he's ever met.

And it works.

C24. *My tastes haven't changed. Enough. If I'm no longer the young and tall thick meat that all the old pathetic faggots in the glory hole joints need to suck off first and better and am instead thought of as one among their number who, sadly, doesn't quite understand it yet: Fine. I would never deny that I wasn't dirtied by their own disgusting narcissistic interest in the first place.*

24. Do you feel controlled by your sexual desire?

According to police, after the dog refused to fight, Henigan and Thomas poured gasoline over the animal and ignited it.

The brother managed to extinguish the flames, but the dog was so badly burned that he had to be killed, Benjamin said.
(TEEN GETS JAIL IN DOG'S DEATH, Chicago Tribune, August 20, 1999)

C25. *My choices have formed me. Formed around me. Infected me and reduced me.*

25. Do you ever think your sexual desire is stronger than you are?

I like saying "Thank You". And I like it a lot when the other idiot says it. I always watch very carefully. I look very closely.

About a week after I first heard about the tiny little case, the August 20, 1999 *Chicago Sun Times* continued the story as JAIL FOR TEEN WHO HELPED INJURE DOG:

Terrance Henigan, 17, is sorry he helped set his little brother's puppy on fire, but he's still going to jail.

The Lawndale teen has given his 12-year-old

102

brother a new dog and has been forgiven, the boy's sister said Thursday after Henigan was sentenced to six months in Cook County Jail.

C26. *I am older and know that options I never wanted are no longer open to me. A supposed vicious circle of less options and less access all carmelized by desperation and a staunch and stupid refusal to move the fuck on. To grow up and die by the choice you wouldn't make again if you could only rethink it all and take maybe some of it back.*

Questions 1–25 from pages 93–96 and questions 1–19 from pages 127 and 128 of THE MURDER OF CHILDHOOD, Ray Wyre & Tim Tate, Penguin, London, 1995.

1. Tell me what you did. I'm not going to interrupt this time. I'm just going to let you speak.

All I did was watch. As her mother taught her how to put on make-up over the cuts and bruises that her father had caused all over her tiny face. It'll be fun, her mother told her to try and get her mind off the damage. We'll play dress up.

I started to masturbate. All I did was masturbate. Me touching myself. I knew that at some point the child would want to see how her face looked in a mirror. With all the new make-up on. And then she would see the new red scars and pain underneath. And as soon as I realized that would happen. When I anticipated that shock of tears and flush. That child swell of pure unprotected rage and powerlessness. Even though I only saw the mother dabbing pink blush and waxing red lips and pinching and cooing all over the little beaten beatable child's cute welled nature; I started to feel an ugly strong pulse inside my cock, safely fastened tight underneath my dirty stained button-fly jeans.

The mother licked her finger and poked it into a small round pat of brown. Then she brushed the wet paint in soft strokes over the small terrorized face of the thinking hard first grader. You could see the sensation of the child was all on the touch of the mother. She needed to be comforted more than dollied.

I slipped my hand over my pants, under my belly, and grabbed the outline of my pressing hard-on. I tried to pull it up and fix it from straining and hurting against my pants. I massaged my hard packed balls and worked around my shaft. Getting thick and long and responding to her childish lips and tears and lessons and abused father crushed and fleshed out nightmares all stinging her games and new mama words and squeaky questions.

Mom brushed the girl's long tangled mousey hair back and tied it in a pony tail with a rubberband. Always sleek and messy and now out of the way for today's clown job. The mother must have registered her hatred over the child's state or, at least, her own miserable life as its second most important cause. But she hid it all perfectly.

I decided to undo my buttons and let my cock poke out straight from my jeans and shorts. I shovelled my balls out as well. Like some teenager. Like some rapist nigger slob. I felt like a dog and sunk into rubbing myself up and down. Little cunt. Little beaten up child. Fucked in her girly face forever now. She'll grow up bent and hurting and screaming like just before in her bedroom for her tall dad to leave her alone, leave her alone, mommy, mommy, help, as his huge drunk worker's hands slap her full in her chubby face and slash at her cheeks and cut hard into her big soft lips.

And the mother won't put the fucking lipstick on quick enough. Old stupid cunt. Old idiot bag full of herself and worn by her age and failures and her nonsense womanly needs and distractions and cheap wishes. Her wizened mother unplugged tits. Her stretch marks that that new bawling hymen carved out of her on the way into that lie both fully grown sentient adults skunked long ago.

You don't see those marks and cuts on your gut and above your old meated cunt and on the sides of your pruned nipples and dugs as part of you, do you, mother? The way you see that bleeding wreck contorting into tears and cycles and Max-factor. The ugly beaten rag doll with a voice now still looking for your sucked out sagged in tit. Or do you, hippie? Do you see it as all part of the wondrous plan and design like the new hairs on your lip and cheeks and navel and the peeling walls inside your hung vagina and the new spread of your deep dimpled ass and fallen hips. The body your child abusing mate can't stand. The one he doesn't agree with. The words you can't find to teach him. To convince him. To fool him. And yourself. And your ripped up little baby.

She deserves it.

She deserved a lot more.

The mother over the child. The child especially.

A young boy imagining that he wants to suck on somebody's cock like one of the boys in his algebra class goes home to his mom's make-up box. He wakes up mornings sleeping on his stomach and, first thing, sees

himself not being able to wait to have his ass pumped full of hurting spreading dripping cock. He outlines his kissed lips in dark eyebrow pencil and colors in the pursed wretched pink space in as bright a red as his mother buys to show his fantasy boyfriend where to stick it.

I took him home when he grew older. I met him at a video rental shop that dedicated its entire second floor to pornography. Since I was renting transsexual videos – thinking Matthew Shepherd to be close enough at that time – he asked me if I lived nearby. No. But he did.

He put on lipstick and a long black goth wig which I made him take off. I didn't want to cum in the mouth of a would-be woman. I wanted to fuck a slight man wearing lipstick around the area I deposited my sick filth in.

D. WHAT IS YOUR ELEMENT?

D1. *You can try and control yourself. Your whole life. But controlling the world outside your body and your repulsive anti-social urges and sublimations will always prove far more difficult. So you become a creep. Or, you remain a creep.*

2. Hang on, let's not go too fast. Were you able to distinguish at that time whether she was unconscious or dead? Or what did you think?

The child had her face beaten. I couldn't see her frail hurted body. A diner down the street from me sports a short little mess with constantly raccooned eyes as if her significant other – as likely to be a lesbian as it is to be a speeded drunk semi-employed truck driver – beats her face down into the warped tiled kitchen floor weekly.

It doesn't make me hard.

It doesn't make my grilled cheese and coffee any better or make me tip a couple quarters more.

The little girl doesn't begin to know better until when?

A welfare mother spends her court kid's cereal

money on new brands of cover possibilities as much to change her look and her slim chances to corrupt someone new, as she does to feel a little better, a little cleaner, a little more special about herself and her previous bad choices.

A hooker on video allows herself to be cummed on one after another by at least twenty-five men collected from within the porn industry and various nearby bus stations. There is virtually no connective or penetrative sex. The prostitute is first paid to masturbate herself in front of the shirtless underwear clad men who sit waiting for their quick shots at her face only. Then they strip off in unison and start to masturbate. When they're ready to cum they frantically struggle to fit their orgasms to the director's sense of frame and deposit the shooting dribbling sperm on the prostitute's face. Which is incrementally covered in ever thickening wads of sliding sticking puddling cum. The idea is to let the cum collect and coagulate. The girls are not cleaned or toweled off until all who can cum do. Each girl is paid to kneel and face up to the acts.

In the American *Bukkake* series there are usually three women to each one and a half hour edited tape. Each woman has her own vignette. Some of the women hold glasses and cups, even a lollipop, under their mouths and chins to catch the overflowing cum that runs down their cocked faces like, pick one, sticky bun frosting or sick white globs of thick snot.

At the end, the filthied beast who sometimes catches the odd load directly into her mouth but most times keeps her lipsticked gump shut tight except to spit out the blotches of cum that collect at the sides of her seeping smile, gets rinsed off by buckets and jugs of water.

The actual minutes of the videos are made of anonymous cocks being furiously self-massaged and spurting on the classless beast's face and tattooed or pierced or sloppily implanted breasts. And all her make-up. The faces of the men are kept well out of camera shot; mostly being male navel to thigh to her face and neck and hair-do. Low rent. Ladies.

The videos are sold off the back of exploitive

advertising wildly suggestive of, but perfectly absent of, real misogyny. The back drop is that these women are compensated and, although so many so-called porn stars wouldn't allow themselves to perform such obviously degrading acts, these girls who aren't cute or conventionally beautiful enough to make it to the rarefied hypertrophied heights of porn starlet-dom and extra picks and choices, do, in fact, make the best of the situation available to them. After all. What do they care. It's just cum. And they don't get fucked out and stretched up like endless anal scenes do to the big girls. And they don't have to swallow any of the cum. Like the so very pretty regulars on Howard Stern do. The audience wants to see it spat out and dripping into full oily coverage. It's all cash and easy semantics and inhibited losers and a perfect way to exploit the current unfriendly trends of perfectly safe male stupidity and what god gave you and natural spiritual bodily freedoms.

They're above it all. I guarantee you.

D2. *The market for videos like Gang Bang Angels and especially the American Bukkake series must be mainly in the repressed cock hound demographic. They seem perfect for those men frightened or resentful of their burgeoning, closeted or fully denied homosexuality. Greasy cocks on cocks with little or no personality except size and masturbating idiosyncrasies. And a more than approachable woman made to expose the inner sow she rotates upon and tries to hide so badly. She pays for female pulling power and access and oafish male lust and possibly even the lazy viewer's own wavering and jealous gender confusion. All those fat cocks. Convenient polymorphous perversities and paraphilias. And it ends with her looking worse in simple natural urges.*

3. Were you frightened she might be dead?

And the thinly scripted videos like *Gang Bang Angels* that feature spitting and slapping but no broken tree branches or fists or stopped hard cum shots directly cleanly into the

throats of would-be beating cutting victims or into the sight fading wombs of future black abortives: The women easily convince themselves and lower their expectations to the level of the sweaty loser with the most money in his hand. Fine. If that's what you think they want. I don't mind. I really don't think you're strong enough.

D3. *In Gang Bang Angels #3, a behind the scenes addendum displays the only actress getting her make-up applied. This volume goes a bit further in cleaning up the action that has just passed. Showing the actress and the eight or so actors getting the pre-film prep from the director and his solicitations of preference instructions from the actress. She's concerned about fingers in her asshole and scratching. There's a quick friendly poll taken of what men will agree to have their asses eaten by her and lots of reassurances to just have fun.*

4. So, whether she was unconscious or dead, what did you do then? You took the pants off her, and then what did you do when you stood over her?

Gang Bang Angels #4 includes among the final credits a series of out-takes from the single day's shooting: The prostitute heading up the stairs behind the set, having finished her eight men or so suck and DP fuck day job, and into the showers. She removes her long blonde fall with some difficulty and passes one of the lesser paid buff studs drying off his cock and stomach as she reaches beyond him to turn on the water. Also included among the montage is footage of her having her make-up applied by a rented professional and a stage hand bringing in a small pint of Cuervo Tequila which he presents to the cameraman mock surreptitiously. As if it mattered.

D4. *The setting for Gang Bang Angels #3 is a bar with a large pool table and a stage. The actress pretends she's acting out a fantasy about fucking all the men there. And begins by sucking off a couple of guys at the bar. She starts off on the floor, then on the pool table, ends up on*

the stage, back to the pool table, etc. She has two big
thick cocks slid into her slimy cunt at the same time.
Slowly. Carefully. Patiently. Even gently. And then one oiled
cock after another slobs their pissing cum into her face and
tonguing mouth.

5. Where did you ejaculate?

I beat myself off harder and faster as I wait for the lipstick.
To cover that little deep slice in the center of her fat child
chewed lower lip. This is where daddy hit you and cut you
and I want to fuck you. The way he said he's sorry and the
way you need to listen and believe and the headache I
want to split into fucking deeper pornography images over
memories. I want her flatter and waiting on the floor of
my bathroom.

D5. *During the behind the scenes footage, the actress*
confesses to the exact same motivation as the character
she's supposed to be playing. That having sex with so
many men all at the same time has been a fantasy of hers
for a long time and making this movie will, luckily, finally
fulfil that personal dream.

6. On the floor? So she was still unconscious at that time?

A long fat forefinger and an old bent thumb pulled
alongsides of a tiny bald vagina to open it up; see how far
it could spread and what it would look like. The digits
pressed in and squeezed the chubby flesh as hard in as it
would stretch. The cunt was dry. As in not cummed in or
on, rather than naturally unlubricated as the child was
obviously far younger than even prepubescent. This would
be the position to investigate the damage wrought on any
such childish organ. To see if there were any immediate
entry scratches or vicious bites or the faint red burns of a
too large adult cock or finger or wooden tool or mass-
market plastic dildo having been shoved too thick, too
long, too quick, too unready, too uncaring into the minute

space just beyond that barely formed, barely folded, tight shut opening.

The fingers would peel that tiny tot's cunt open to see what would fit. So far. And what wouldn't and guess at the damage it might cause, the trail it might leave and the suddenly sobering possibilities of intense public outrage and the crush an arrest and life sentence a child raper, and murderer, would have to endure. And would this be worth it. This little cunt attached to a little mouth and flat flesh stretched politely over such small brittle bones and miniature blushes and games and tears and eyes.

It never was innocent. Unless innocence means dumb. It was barely human. Too few years here. And there's no need to twist the little pig into something less than real: inside that disastrously planned little hole lies all the exact same minutiae that'll grow up and turn and mold into all the other wonderful possibilities of female-dom and motherhood and great accomplishments and sisterly sense. It's all there now. Painted with the rules and guides of its absent parents and blossoming into them cancerous knot by knot.

No matter what kind of parents they are. The kind who didn't wrap the cocoon warm enough or the kind that didn't care enough not to unlock the house doors no matter how far past teenage curfew it was. Or the kind, most usually black, who'll sell anything they can find or create for this very minute's money to buy some crack, heroin or soda pop and corn chips.

This cunt is small. And still so fucking shut tight that the womb that stenches inchoate sunk lapse beneath the pit is all just one small detail in the bigger truth of someone else's cruelty. The body is incomplete. The nature is arrested. The chances were just beginning to show and the flesh ready to register more the damage done to it than the promise created for it.

The man who took the photo – filling the frame with nothing but fingers and child slash – must have been interested in the crime rather than the autopsy. The lack of detail is extreme. The photo is a record of the act the hand performed rather than the budding secrets of a child's

artful fascinating vagina. Though the photo can be a perfect replica of both; the crueller intention certainly seems reflected in the fact that the published reproduction crops in so much finger, so much action. Although the long tips of these aged and clawing fingers may be included to give size to the comparatively very small, very young cunt. Below the important paedophiliac demarcation of ten years. And it is altogether even more possible that there were not two men in the room when this shot was taken. In the hotel room. Which would have been best. One hard-on'd rapist to hold the little bawling duct taped fuckable rat down and then spread her wriggling baby cunt as far as baby sex flesh would spread between his two dirty smelling like her guts fingers, while the other fucker sits across from the sexualized sweaty rape and snaps as many photos as he can before he needs to jam his own fingers into the little death before she dies or stops crying and faints and ruptures and begs even one more long hard jacking pumping cock squeezing second.

Hold her down.

Tighter. Hold her head back.

One fuck at her baby feet, the other at her baby blonde head; two naked lazy slobs with full engorged adult genitalia and wrinkles and spots and skin tags and heated plans all over, towering, forcing, cajoling, laughing, shadowing the tiniest little four- or five- or six-year-old girl sat forever in the darkened middle.

One hand stretches the cunt open before the inside walls rip, as far outside as the pork flesh will allow before breaking into evidence. Another hand holds her tiny wrists together, rubbing mean, between five pushing and pulling determined fingers. His cock shaking and jutting all over her last use of eyes and burning brain and denial mechanisms and memory. Another set of hands encourages position. Masturbates and grinds and pokes and deftly records by the small plastic and metal camera like mom and dad used on attention soaking holidays and acting lessons.

D6. *I don't know that it really matters. Having had my cock*

up some nigger hooker's alcohol sopped throat and then,
just a few hours later, sticking it unwashed up a nice high
schooler's face

7. But was she unconscious or dead?

Alternatively: one man with one hand around the special
naked darling's filthy clean cunt and the other hand on his
camera. He may have her sat in front of him, so that his
probing hand and arm are bent up and pointed down at
the elbow. His head down and staring at his work. He
might have her laid down flat beneath him, his heavy fat
weight and hairy manhandled balls and slung strange
frightening penis dangling back and forth into her baby
fresh face. A bouncing thick cock glistening at the tip with
seeping disgusting dollops of drooling pre-cum. Ready, by
dint of mother nature, to wet any hole regardless of its
own design or interests.

D7. *The high school girl who turned into a quiet married*
friend, who now owns a sandwich shop in a trendy part of
town, must have loads of sexual experiences behind her.
And sucking some dumb kid's cock that may have tasted
like the spit of a drunk black human wreck can hardly be
seen as an extreme low point.

8. You didn't know which, or it didn't matter, because you still carried on with the behavior. What did you do when you stood over her?

Have you ever masturbated with child pornography?
         The way one is meant to? For the reason it is
created? The difficulty in obtaining it, the dangers in even
owning it, the sickness one has to trundle through to come
to one small barely realized desire.
         With a fucking magazine. The manufactured and
professionally reproduced and planned issues like the
European INCEST 4. The only one the police took from me.
         Or with videos. Or with five minute 8mm films.
The way I did when I was much younger. The kind I used

to buy from a faggot paedophile out of his gold coast basement in Chicago. Who I met while pursuing an entirely different form of entertainment.

D8. *It tasted better that way. It's not like she was doing it for herself anyways. Big deal. That's not when she got herpes. It doesn't matter now because it didn't really matter then.*

9. Looking at her?

From the Brief And Appendix for Peter Sotos, Appeal To The Supreme Court Of Illinois:
Section 11-20.1 (a) (2) makes criminal the mere possession of child pornography. The State claims that the statute is a valid attempt by the State to protect its children by prohibiting even the private possession of child pornography. The State contends that it has a compelling interest in protecting its children which overcomes this defendant's right to privacy within his home. This is so, the State argues, because the value of child pornography is "de minimus".

D9. *Before AIDS drastically and slowly changed the tenor of glory hole joints and backroom sex booths, it was a common thrill among crawling fags to suck on twenty or so different cocks a night. All the spit and old dirty fists and diseases and amyl and sweat and cheese collected in the mouths and throats of men who crept and spread from shared cock to cock. The idea was unclean. The STDs crumbling away over horny years at immune systems and the wear and tear always starting to show earlier than it should.*

10. So you masturbated as she was laid there on the floor, unconscious or dead, and her skirt up around her waist and her knickers were off?

It's just one small part of one small girl. In a high contrast black and white snap done in extreme close-up. And if it

This is what I remember.

These are the names I give the little cunts and cocks I saw in magazines and films and slides and accounts being molested in ways feminists, psychiatrists, sociologists, reporters, cops, victims, parents and paedophiles explained to me.

D10. *Imagine being so pathetic as to wrench your own psychotic jollies out of acts so unimportant to others. As if you're the only one who got the joke that the entire room only finds ...embarrassing.*

11. Why would they only charge you with lewd and libidinous behavior for what was clearly an attempted murder?

JonBenet's cunt.

Matthew Shepard's mouth.

Ryan Harris' life.

The hookers and stolen playthings look for new words to describe what they feel is their soul. That schizoid chimera best employed to wash the filth of guilt and childhood confusion right back down the throats of those caught up in decisions that slowly decay whatever lofty designs they've used up all their lives until then. Until the moments when they come to realize: This is what this hole is for. This is who owns the hole. And it makes god forsaken sense to sell it back to them.

A little girl with long curly black hair to her shoulders and in her big brown eyes looks at the camera lens she was directed to and slowly sings a counting song. She's wearing a print country-style dress in a warm country-style room in, no doubt, a big safe country-style wood and brick ranch home.

The cameraman moves in while she sings, so by the end of the commercial I'm left with just her soft white cheeks and pouty child mouth and little nose and large eyes all gently framed by that soft black hair. The bottom of the screen frame, however, intrudes even more violently as the little safe face gets bigger and closer. Perfectly. As it

details what makes this little, maybe six-year-old, raven so much more special than any typical degenerate paedophile focus:

"This is Kate
Her stepfather forces sex on her
He says he'll hurt her mother
If she tells"

She's got pretty white teeth and she smiles to show them as the commercial ends. "1-800-4-A-CHILD. CHILDHELP USA. KEEP THE LINES OPEN."

Geraldo Rivera was kind enough to include this and various other PSAs concerning child sexual abuse as part of the "Exposing The Last Taboo" episode of his eponymous daytime talk show.

Broadcast about seven months after JonBenet Ramsey was murdered, Geraldo used JonBenet's case to highlight the need for understanding the disaster to children that is sexual molestation and, apparently, murder.

Geraldo explained his case at the outset: "I think the way to abolish the last taboo is to expose it." To which, his special guest Marilyn Van Derbur Atler gilded: "There is no way to change it unless we understand it."

Marilyn is a wrinkled, oddly tight, smartly dressed, prim looking, white haired old former Miss America who as "advisor to prosecution in JonBenet case" has appeared on countless TV and radio talk shows and news programs detailing her own abuse at the hands of her millionaire father since the age of five. She talks regularly about the help she provided the attorneys investigating JonBenet's murder as related to her own pageant status and incest survivor status.

She often serves to remind one of what rich pampered molested barbie dolls will grow into if allowed to make it past the age of six, perhaps.

D11. *So you shove your make-believe tentacles out even further. And for anything to work it has to end in a victim. AIDS brings all the filthy forgettable sex acts back into perspective. Sex becomes just as wretched as you quietly always knew it would be. And luck replaces guilt.*

12. What does it feel like when you tell me you're in a dark place, in an air-raid shelter, with a little girl? How old was she?

Every week since JonBenet's death comes another crop of tabloids most often with a shot of and a garish blurb about the little made-up pre-six-year-old on the cover. *The Globe*, one of the four main tabloids, is virtually consistent. Every weekly issue for almost two years has had a feature, with pictures, of the bright red lip'd little doll.

And every week I pick through and buy the tabloids with the articles and photos of her. Available everywhere. I cut out the pictures and check the context and keep them in private files. I'm quick to remove the JonBenets from the supermarket celebrity crap that surrounds her and slide her back into my own specific context. Where I use her as pornography.

Marilyn Van Derbur Atler: "The average age of a child violated for the first time is six."

Geraldo Rivera: "Really? That's how old JonBenet Ramsey is. Was."

D12. *And you barely expand your narrowing vision into reference points and touch stones. And you're helped along. The victims so pained at being alone and forgotten huddle into desperate groups, call them communities, and start to howl and scratch more violently now as symbols and examples. Their noise and details and documentations disseminate larger traumas made from smaller and smaller infractions. And it's not supposed to doubleback on the lepers. But it always does. Making the initial pain so much more bloated now. At the same time she is encouraged to dig deep for the future relief of personal enlightenment and overcoming and empowerment. Which are all just lies.*

All these rape victims and family members of murdered losses collecting and sifting and petitioning and briefing and getting filmed. The unique and unfair ordeals melting into opportunities to educate the dumb public about everything from everyday sexism to the intricacies of the legal system to finding your own little hidden bird's

voice.

13. Seven. And you may have killed her. What does that feel like?

Fourteen-year-old Kandace, a seventh grader, who Geraldo's been letting tell her story, wants to read a poem to her father.

> "What you've done, I can't undo.
> Times you molested me, I can't forget about you.
> I feel so dirty, yet I'm clean.
> I take a bath but it sticks like glue.
> How you disgraced me; how could you do this.
> I was just a little innocent girl without a clue."

Geraldo tells her: "It's lovely. It really is lovely."

At the end of the show he lets Kandace have another minute for a personal message to her father. Geraldo tells her to look straight into the camera. And Kandace tells the cameraman about how she's got friends now and that they'll help her if he – the father, the lens – ever touches her or anyone again:

> "You're not gonna have a (bleep) left."

The propriety that pervades such brutal truths, and, more importantly, the noble need to expose such brutality, is one that all of us, paedophiles and avengers, quickly learn to operate around. The dreaded point makes it through the wire and the details that heat more intensely in your brain than in your ears will just have to do.

D13. *And now you want to see this actress, who puts an even greater amount of herself into her part than what you normally would have suspected. Again. And the only actor who leans down to kiss her after fucking her face is the one wearing the black SUCK IT BITCH t-shirt. And you tear through all you know about the acts and monies and politics and roles and reasons and you settle for the Krista Absalon case.*

A black and white photo of aging Krista graced the cover of the November/December issue of MS. (volume 5, number 3) under the politely superimposed:

**14. And you were scared. But what did it feel as you
were masturbating watching it? Very excited? You
must have done.**

Slow motion shots of little JonBenet modelling down the
runway during one of her little miss beauty pageants. Her
child face all done up in make-up the way her mother
would wear. The lipstick on her baby lips target all the sex
she doesn't understand yet forever. Over the footage of
this little made-up bag of bones and lessons comes a
stuttering voice recorded over a phone line. Adult. Female.

"I was molested by my grandfather as far back as I
can remember till I was thirteen years old. I never told
anyone.

I always wanted attention 'cause that's all I
thought I was good for."

It turns out that "Anne" had called the Geraldo
show to offer her thoughts, personal revelations and
disturbances over a recent broadcast about JonBenet.
"Anne" wanted to let the Geraldo show know that she
thought someone should check out "any male people in
(JonBenet's) life" and especially John Ramsey because "it
really bothers me."

The footage of JonBenet displaying her kiddie
wares cuts to "Anne", 29, now sitting on the panel and
broken down in tears next to 14-year-old Kandace.
Geraldo was so touched by her confession of personal pain
that he offered her a chance to tell, live on his show, more
people than just a private recorded phone line manned by
TV producers. About herself. And others just like her.
About JonBenet. Except still living.

And, as it turned out, while not a beauty queen,
"Anne" was a failed entertainer who could blame her lust
for fame on the abuse she suffered.

One grows accustomed to the specious
connections that those who have suffered through abuse

make to the abuse that hopefully little Jonbenet has suffered. It is somewhat more acceptable when the details are immediately juxtaposed, or even better, read over the top of pageant footage.

D14. *From Journey To Justice by Natalia Rachel Singer (MS., IBID):*

Krista *had* come home feeling "sore and wet", she said, but since she had wanted to drink herself numb – and succeeded – she assumed that's why she didn't suspect anything initially. She would later tell her lawyer, "I wrote the pain off to my period, but the truth is, I was too sick to pay attention to anything." Within a few weeks, Krista developed chlamydia, a sexually transmitted disease.

15. How long did you squeeze her throat for?

Rose West would sit on a couch across from her husband Fred and spread wide her legs. Look at that, she'd say addressing her splayed open cunt to her husband's attention. I bet you wish you had something to fill that up, she'd say, or something approximate. And Fred would love it. He and she were in on the same joke. His wife spending most of her day fucking nigger after nigger in the hopes of finding bigger and bigger cocks.

There was a book of photos the husband and wife kept, one of many such albums and videos devoted to their personal dedication to sexual documentation. And this particular one was specifically concerned with shots of Rose's cunt in various stages of slack opened and raw fucked-ness.

Cunts get that way, don't they.

And it doesn't necessarily have to come from sitting on the wrong ends of jungle sized nigger dicks minute after minute, does it.

Because these old whores age badly. Don't they. Those old beaten horses, drooping sagging pinched flesh and craters and divots and pits, age into widened folded and hung slabs around which bodies still convinced of some small sense of worth, try and smile and tuck and

primp the ways they did back when they were firm at eighteen, firmer at fourteen. And they still don't get it. Do they.

A review in *AVN* (*The Adult Video News*, October 1998) for the video *Deep Throat Debi* doesn't go half way to describing what really goes on in the 74 minute amateur porn video:

The formula for this four-scene video is simple: Debi blows a well-hung black man for several minutes, then he fucks her in multiple positions and comes on her face. The sex isn't bad, but the couple is so determined to let us know how much they really enjoy themselves that hubby comes from behind the camera and does an impression of a zamboni, licking the jizz off her face and chest in broad circles.

Debi is a pock-mark riddled skull on a withered rag body closer to the disaster side of a middle aged white trash crack whore. Her ass is flab mottled with cellulite and while her gangly frame is abused skinny, her tits even sag deflated under the weight of huge pruned brown nipples and various faded tattoos.

The effect is less:

The action is kept at a steady pace throughout the video with good camera work and very enthusiastic participants.

And more: fat niggers getting sucked off by a garbaged hooker who may like her job just a little more due to her size queen husband who gets off sucking the nigger cum out of her distended cunt and licking it off her grizzled face.

D15. *There's a photo of the main roon of the Casablanca, the bar and restaurant in Gouveneur, NY, where 23-year-old Krista was gang raped by five men. There's no pool table or a small band stage like the one that the actress from Gang Bang Angels #3 gets her fantasy fuck filled. There's no pinball machine from Jodie Foster's award winning ACCUSED performance.*

16. Did she struggle when you did that?

I like the word "little" best. I like the way it gets attached to specific names and cases by anonymous and/or cloying men in professional capacities.

The commercial that immediately preceded the first show that Gordon Elliot did on the JonBenet murder case featured the title "WHAT HAPPENED TO LITTLE JONBENET RAMSEY" stapled over frozen stills of the 6-year-old's little adult painted baby face.

And wrapped inside was another favorite surprise. Little JonBenet got her little dead body dissected by Gordon's special kid-gloved guest Marc Klaas. There's no better way to fuck a little child than to have her parents do it for you. And there's no better way to watch fucked children than to watch someone who knows how to keep fucking it just right. Someone who knows what happens and how it works and what it looks like and what it'll sound like when he opens his gump to say the words that only he can pick out so carefully.

Marc Klaas brings with him all the loud details of his cause. The cause that he has dedicated his new life to now that his daughter is gone. And through the foundation he and his wife run out of his home, appearing on talk shows to enlighten the viewing communities about the best way to protect your children is but one important facet.

From WHO KILLED POLLY? by Frank Spiering (Monterey press, 1995):

Petitioner removed his sweatshirt, opened a condom wrapper, and unrolled the condom onto his penis. He then gathered the nightgown under the victim's armpits and inverted her white mini-skirt over her hips and pelvis, pushing it up her body. Whether petitioner ultimately ejaculated is unknown: the victim's body had decomposed to a point where forensic testing for penetration was not possible; any semen that might have been present in the condom may have been washed away by the elements; and during police interrogation, petitioner himself said only, 'You guys soon find that out.'

D16. *From the same article in MS.:*

"Sue Buckley called me and said, 'I have a girl who heard through rumours that some guys had sex with her while she was unconscious. She doesn't know anything about it.'" Potter told Buckley she ought to interview the men.

17. What do you think?

The best way to masturbate is to use someone else's head. Faggots who need to suck any cock that comes their way and nigger drunk or cranked whores who need to suck any cock that comes their way. Compulsion, for inclusion, for inversion, for sex, for money for more drugs and drink and more poverty back home and nothing else ever better.

Some faggots on their knees in glory holed peep show booths will put condoms on the cock you give them. They'll reach into their back pockets and ask you if you mind. Nigger whores who don't use condoms are usually very unhealthy just like most of the queers who do their job bareback. Some fags hope you can't get sick by sucking cock and have the medical data about membrane fissures and stomach acids, as well as their penicillin quick fixes to prove it. Some nigger cunts hope to give HIV to you but still don't want your pig's cum in their mouths.

From POLLY KLAAS: THE MURDER OF AMERICA'S CHILD by Barry Bortnick (Pinnacle, 1995):

The position of the body, coupled with Davis' past crimes and the unrolled condom found at Pythian Road led investigators to suspect Polly had been raped or at least molested before death.

That Marc's twelve-year-old daughter Polly watched those fat greasy fingers unroll the condom up that greasy fat cock with her last minutes the way faggots might help or niggers might hide is something you'll never know – definitely – until Richard Allen Davis can be trusted enough to tell you and Marc Klaas.

Mr. Klaas offers up sympathy for Mr. and Mrs. Ramsey:

"These people are in the worst emotional state anybody can be in. They're in a place that often times,

people are not able to get out of. They're in a dark room looking for a way out. And some times people don't find a way out."

But Mr. Klaas basks in more virtue than he'll allow the newest famous parents of a murdered child on the block:

"I think it's a type of psychological child abuse. Is what I think. Six-year-olds should not be sexually provocative."

That warm mouth and the tongue technique or hard sucking jaws or whatever the beast on the sloppy end of your cock brings to the party is rendered largely blank by the tight latex covering your hard-on. Which is perfect. You have to look down to see what to feel. Their knees in filth, their inability to do anything else, their ghetto sale, their pock-holes and drug rot, their twelve-year-old face that left nighttime make-up stains on the hood when placed over her head.

Gordon Elliot continues to draw out Marc's informed opinions on the likes of a six-year-old parading around in clothes designed for older, more world weary whores. "It eroticized her," Gordon says. "She's playing barbie," he forgives and then suggests that he knows the secret to eroticizing something:

"There's a lot of people in this country who look at these little babies in a very different light."

Marc adds his personal pain to the mix again: "Beautiful little girl." And "Who knows what she would have been when she grew up." And finally:

Gordon: "You sound like you're talking about Polly."

Marc: "Well, I am, aren't I?"

D17. *And:*

Were it not for the villager's love of gossip, Krista would never have known she had been assaulted. But the stories some people continue to tell about her are brutal, cruel tales about a woman who stepped out of line. Rumours circulate that Krista has group sex in cars; that the night of the gang rape, she was performing oral sex on

126

men lined up outside the bar. In Gouverneur, many people consider Krista a trouble-maker or, worse, a money-hungry sex fiend.

18. What do you think? What's your guess?

Both Geraldo and Leeza invited family members and friends of the little raped and beaten black girl known as Girl X onto their respective programs. Both talk show hosts wanted to confront the possible racist inequities of the media and public by discussing the relative lack of attention the crime against Girl X received when it occurred the very same Christmas week as the murder of JonBenet.

Girl X had been left for dead. By a stranger that raped and beat her retarded in a stairwell of the Cabrini Green Housing Projects in Chicago. She was nine years old, a fourth grader and lived in one of the most notorious housing projects in the US. And she lived. So the crimes against the children were virtually the same.

Geraldo: "I know that the girl was found with the gang graffiti scrawled on her abused and violated body."

Geraldo also had the good sense to show footage of one of Girl X's school friends screaming in tears at the bottom of one of the dirty rusted project stairwells having just received the news about the rape and brutal beating.

And while Leeza's guests moaned about the media being so accustomed to black on black crime that the rape registered nary a blip on the national level, Geraldo made sure his audience knew it was a big story in Chicago by interviewing the newscasters and reporters who brought the locals as much information as was allowed.

Unlike JonBenet, Girl X was by law protected from being named or identified by whatever footage could be found of a typical little black girl growing up in the projects. And while bitching about the racism inherent in the lack of even general coverage, it didn't escape the attention of most that Leeza and Geraldo still had to tag the black on black crime onto the footage of lily white

JonBenet.

The sad reality is that Girl X's life makes better copy. But newscasters can't call her project poverty no chance life miserable because of all the others sharing that life and watching it on TV at what would be the same time. JonBenet's life is better pornography because it is what is allowed.

D18. *At the start of The World's Biggest Anal Gang Bang, the actress is filmed getting her hair done, preparing for her role. The actress – whose name I do remember, Brooke Ashley – is sitting in a make-up chair listening to her stylist's concern over her client's job to get fucked by what was then fifty men, mainly, in her asshole:*
"Wow. Whoa. You think you'll be alright?"
Brooke assures her that she's up for it. And just before the scene breaks, the camera pans down to Brooke's open white robe where she is seen to be rubbing her clit.

19. Can you see her face?

On Geraldo's primetime cable talk show – more respectably upmarket, investigative and, on the surface, less tabloid-y – *Rivera Live*, Geraldo married a couple of JonBenets with Ryan Harris and Sherrice Iverson. Two other little black girls raped and murdered under glamorous circumstances. However, as Geraldo soon started to obsess over the Clinton/Lewinski blow-job the public who had come to rely on Geraldo was robbed of their best chances.

D19. *Contrary to the advertising, Brooke Ashley's gang-bang is much more genteel than the previous examples in the genre. The men enter her one at a time, one on one, with no great long lines of gawking, genital tugging non-industry strangers all waiting for their brief stab at tearing her tiny ass apart. Some of the men wear condoms as they dig into her cunt and then her asshole. While others don't. Some of the actors exit the actress' anus only to jerk themselves off and aim their cum directly into her slightly*

128

slacker asshole. In one brief moment, and it's hard to tell, but one of these incidents ends with Brooke pushing away from a just spent actor as he looks to be trying to sink his cum soaked cock back into her asshole. Brooke Ashley, the actress, and her asshole.

20. What I'm finding amazing, I suppose, is when we talked about Laura, and your fantasy concerning Laura, that in a sense it was like a re-enactment of what you just told me. I mean what is actually going on? Do you find that an unconscious side of you takes over, that bypasses intellectual thinking, or what?

Christopher Meyer. Ten years old.
        The photo I keep of him (clipped from the *Chicago Sun-Times*) is the same one Geraldo kept showing. And the footage of him playing in a living room before he was murdered comes courtesy of Geraldo's special show on child predators.

D20. As part of the TRUE LIFE series produced by MTV, an episode entitled "I'M A PORN STAR" aired on October 7, 1998 and featured, among its behind the scenes access, an interview with Brooke Ashley.
        Brooke sitting at another make-up table with her hair in curlers, getting ready for either a shoot or a dance. The interview was edited slightly to tighten up her answers and focus as the actress talked directly into the camera. She talked about The World's Biggest Anal Gang Bang (also called "Brooke's All Anal Adventure", Midnight Video):
        "I got a call to do a film and with the amount of money they were offering me I was thinking; god, you know, either this is a great budget for porn or I'm going to be doing something here that you haven't told me about yet."

21. Yeah. Yeah. But what I'm interested in is that it stayed there in your head and that you've had the image of it for a very long time. You may have

struggled with it for a very long time – not wanting, but it kept coming into your head ...it kept coming back.

Geraldo used this show to spotlight the crimes against Christopher, Megan Kanka, Amber Haggerman and Alicia and DeAnn Jones by sandwiching their cases and family pain between updates on the JonBenet case.

D21. *"They wanted me to have sex with a total of 32 men. Okay, sure, that's a lot. That seemed like a lot for me but I was thinking this day and age when you have another person out there that's just as pretty as you are – maybe prettier, maybe fresher – that's willing to do just as much as you, if not more; you just had to keep up with that competition. I felt that this was going to enhance my career."*

22. Yes. Now I also know because the fantasy has been there that sometimes you have been masturbating about other things, that image still comes into your head and you don't like that. You didn't like it over the years, but it was there and you end up guilty and therefore feel bad. Am I right?

Geraldo mentions, before he runs over the Megan Kanka victim details, that her murderer Jesse Timmendequas was facing the first day of his trial that day.

Court TV was allowed to broadcast live only the opening and closing statements in the case. As such, prosecutor Kathryn Flicker faced the jury (who were off camera) and recounted for the watching world Jesse's confession. She read in a brave but disgusted and angry voice, careful to keep it all professional and fair:

"I tried to penetrate her with my penis for about two minutes and I couldn't get it all the way in."

"No matter how hard I tried to force it all the way in, I couldn't get it in because she was too small."

"I tried to penetrate her in her pussy."

"Question. Did you at anytime try to have anal sex with Megan. Answer. No. But I may have slipped when I was trying to penetrate her pussy."

Geraldo had lubed the stage earlier with photos of the little chubby faced seven-year-old and the vivid report on her rape and murder:
　　　　"Once inside he lures her to an upstairs bedroom. Strangles her unconscious with a belt. Rapes her. And asphyxiates her to death with a plastic bag. Then he places her small body into a tool box and drives her to a soccer field two and a half miles away where he dumps her body into the bushes."

D22. *"I was expecting so much from it. And it actually had total opposite impact on my life.*
　　　　(starts to cry slightly)
　　　　"I tried to make it where everybody had to wear condoms but they told me that, um, in the contract that only half of the guys in the movie would be, um, able to wear the condoms and the other half would not.
　　　　"Some of them I've known for a long time. Most of them have known me pretty well because they've been booked in my movies, vice versa. After completion of the movie, I went to go get my blood drawn for my routine every thirty day HIV test. And the following day, I get a really odd voice message. And I call it on the car phone and it says 'Hi baby, um, this is Jim South, honey, this is very important, I need you to not work. Call me on Monday.' My agent! My agent's making money off me working, what's he thinking?
　　　　"I – I get called into the office on Monday. They close the door behind me and I knew something was wrong and basically it was this: I ...tested positive for HIV, um, I think I went into mourning for myself for a period of time. (deep exhale) It's something that ...you're so careful (starts to cry) and you are. You think everybody's tested, you know, you see people's test. How could this happen? I

haven't had sex other than this movie and my boyfriend wears a condom. What's going on here?"

23. And as you masturbate, you connect those images with orgasm. Orgasm is the most powerful experience and internal feeling that you can have. But, connected to that orgasm and fantasy was that behavior. Right? It's okay, you can tell: don't worry about this.

Mika Meyer is invited to talk about her sense of injustice and loss.

"It's dying a thousand deaths everyday. It's walking around with your open heart surgery never being stitched up."

Geraldo had just told the audience about mother Mika's little boy Christopher:

"The little boy had been stabbed 53 times in the chest and the back. His genitals had been completely castrated."

Then he introduced Glenda Hill, the sister of little Tara Sue Huffman, the five-year-old girl that was also murdered by the man who murdered Christopher.

Later, Geraldo would pounce outraged. Timothy Buss had served only twelve years in jail for the murder of Tara Sue and shortly after release murdered little Christopher. And he follows the same tack of brutal caring bravery with Glenda that he did with Mika when he asked her to "remind them about how exactly Timothy Buss murdered your son."

Geraldo: "What did he do to your sister? He didn't just murder her ...."

Glenda: "No. After she was dead he stuck sticks up inside of her body. And... um... he bashed in the front of her face and... he beat her. (starts to cry)"

Geraldo: "He served twelve years. Is that right?"

Cari Meyer, sister to the late little Christopher, sits in the audience and Geraldo walks to her and entreats her to talk about her brother. "It didn't have to be him" she says as the camera swings to Mika who has also now

broken down.

D23. *"I had spent so much of my life. Giving so much of my life to this. And when (sniff) my own business, my own family – people that I spent my thanksgivings with, people that I grew up with. From the time that I was eighteen to twenty-five. Um, I just can not believe our business was in such denial."*

24. I know you have. But you haven't always been able to, have you?

Geraldo continues:
        "A man walking his dog discovers her nude body. Chalky white. Face down. Floating in a creek eight miles from where she had been abducted. Her throat had been slashed five times. Autopsy reports confirm Amber was also sexually molested."
        "Tell us about Amber."
        The mother starts to cry and her face is replaced by a shot of her 9-year-old daughter smiling with jagged teeth and bright blue eyes.
        "She was my dream. She was never in trouble. She did no harm to nobody. She was an innocent little girl."
        A new photo of Amber holding a baby doll sat next to her mother, both smiling, comes on next.
        "How dare that man do this to my little girl. How dare him."

D24. *She cries and the tears run down her previously cum soaked and cock filled mouth. Her lip trembles and at times she seems to have to physically hurl the words out. She twists her tragedy, her bad luck and single worst decision into a condemnation of the business. Which wouldn't have happened before. She asks questions of cosmic inequity and personal confusion and tries to find answers by forcing them into the camera that, once again, records her working so hard.*

25. Yes, and it not only comes back, but at the time masturbation to the fantasy is something that's reinforcing the image. The way you've lived with that. No one has helped you. No one has talked to you. No one has helped you overcome that image... Today, here in this room, you can go back to that cellar, and there in your head is that child, just as real now as it was then. Right?

This is what I've been reduced to.

I've replaced photos and films of children having their pushed up little faces cock fucked and their cookie cutter orifices finger fucked with images of previously safe little darlings smiling before anything special has happened.

Because JonBenet looks prepared and because she smells like she has fucked and killed written all over the inside of her tightest crotch hugging swimsuit if I work hard on the context. What I recognise inside those sold and cropped and considered and financed photos is not so much what she looks like dead and raped but how much she looks like she's got all those fingers on her. Adult fingers and adult mouths clamoring to suck on her 6-year-old cunt; positioning themselves in the midst of an angry hard cock based hard news gang bang.

D25. *And I cum quicker to her tears than I do to her smeared asshole and all the cocks in her femalia and all the whore eyes and invisible infections I could look for. And there's this obnoxious little act that ends perfectly alone and messy and is somehow supposed to stain someone else's reality. But it doesn't. But I breathe it all in and take it with me. I work on the connections, silently and individually, and fish it right back to where it started. With me.*

1. When were you first conscious of the female form, the girl with no hair? When were you conscious of that becoming important to you?

What does a little girl look like. Naked. Vulnerable.

Waiting. Fucked. Crying. Posing for a photo that belongs to an art gallery rather than in my front cock pocket on my way into some glory hole joint.

JonBenet, in no photo I have of her is she belligerent. Or bratty. I have some where she looks away from where she's supposed to and another where she yawns.

I have video footage filmed just a few days before she was murdered, of her singing christmas carols, pretending to blow a sax during the instrumental break and wiggling her little butt. First aired courtesy *American Journal*.

Geraldo played the Ramseys' answering machine message where JonBenet squeaked:

"We're having a great summer. Wish you were here!"

A *60 Minutes* episode, broadcast about five months after JonBenet's death, had a nice introduction to her stage act:

"JonBenet Ramsey!
She'd like to become an Olympic skater.
Her favorite star: Julie Andrews.
JonBenet loves to eat cherries."

D26. *Brooke's life pops up again in an article about porn actress Tricia Devereaux's newly discovered HIV Positive status in the April 1999 issue of POZ:*

Next it was reported that 25-year-old Brooke Ashley – who starred, with 50 men, in *The World's Greatest Anal Gang Bang* – tested positive. In April, long-timer Marc Wallace, who had some 1,500 titles under his belt, including *Anal Anarchy, Anal Savage* and *The Creasemaster*, got the bad news, as did single-name Euro-newcomer Caroline, of *Lewd Conduct, Part 1* fame. May brought word to veteran Kimberly Jade.

2. If you were to place the perfect girl in that chair with you as a target, what would she be? How old would she be?

Nearly seven months after the murder of JonBenet, the Denver investigators were forced to release her (partial) autopsy to the press. The orgy to figure out as close as possible to the truth of whether JonBenet was molested was as thick as the report was vague.

All these well-intentioned vultures targeting this tiny inflamed barely six-year-old dead buried vagina.

Wolf Blitzer sat in for Larry King on his CNN talk show in front of an esteemed panel of reporters, attorneys, a child abuse expert and the ex beauty queen incest victim.

Charlie Brennan (Rocky Mountain News):

"There is very strong indication that she suffered a degree of trauma to the genital area. And it may come down to a matter of semantical discussion as to whether the trauma to the genitals constitutes what we typically call sexual assault or whether that was more under the heading of what we would just call physical abuse. In my book, assault to the genital area – that says sexual assault to me but I think there are obviously a lot of people that may have different interpretations on that."

Bob Grant (Adams County DA and a regular guest on *Rivera Live*) upset for the "human reason" that "intensely personal, private, clinical, graphic detail – not the kind of stuff that you want to hear at your breakfast table" has been released and pored over so meticulously:

"It's just a shame that the memory of this beautiful child has to be sullied with this stuff."

Marilyn Van Derbur Atler seeps into her favorite position and takes Grant to task. She barks again for full disclosure of all the "intimate details" so that the public can learn that "these children are pried open and raped – viciously."

D27. *From the next page:*

Devereaux's genealogy pointed Mitchell directly toward Marc Wallace. Devereaux had worked with him twice in the fall of 1997, and had never worked with the other three women who tested positive; she also says she never shot up drugs and had sex with only one man outside the industry, who's HIV negative.

Soon an industry backlash dubbed Wallace "Patient Zero", and rumours flew that he used needles or did gay outcalls; that he had known he was positive for a year, and forged negative test results.

3. What would she be wearing? Picture her there in the chair, and look at the chair. Put her there.

Dr. Richard Krugman (child abuse expert, University Of Colorado Medical Center – he appeared earlier in the day on MSNBC News, also discussing the autopsy, alongside Robert Ressler, the serial killer profiler expert.):
"...and at the same time she had several other fresh abrasions, scratches, bruises on her body including an abrasion on her hymen that was part of what was found at the autopsy. Whether all these occurred at the same time as, shortly after, shortly before, I think is not clear from reading the autopsy."
Wolf Blitzer: "Is there in your opinion, and you're an expert in this kind of area, is there enough to conclude that JonBenet Ramsey was sexually abused?"
Wolf Blitzer: "When we're talking about sexual abuse, are we talking about sexual abuse on the night of the murder or is there any evidence in this autopsy report that suggests there was previous sexual abuse?"

D28. *Luke Ford, author of A History Of X (100 Years Of Sex In Film), runs a porn industry gossip website and recently published an interview with Marc Wallace:*
Luke: "Brooke Ashley says she asked you if you knew you were HIV positive, and you were silent."
Marc: "She never asked me that. No one can ever prove that I knew. They didn't ask me or find out from the treatment center."
Luke: "Supposedly Patrick Collins asked you the same question and you were silent."
Marc: "No, why would I be silent?"
Luke: "Because it's an insulting question."
Marc: "Well, yeah. I'd say, 'fuck you. You're an asshole. If you can't figure that out for yourself, I'm not going to

answer it'."

<u>About two years ago, Marc and Brooke did cocaine and ecstasy at Tom Byron's house. Marc and Brooke had sex while doing the drugs.</u>
<u>Marc: "If I had it then, she would've had it way back then. Some other girls too that I partied with..."</u>

4. Short? Long? What sort of colour?

John Gibson sat in for Geraldo Rivera on *Rivera Live* that same night. Another group of criminal attorneys, reporters and medical experts were gathered to pick apart the newest glance at that little paper cunt.

Among the details that Gibson directed attention to were the urine stained long underwear and the mysterious red stain on the panties the child had on when she was found dead by her father.

John Gibson: "Does that red stain mean anything in particular?"

Craig Silverman (civil and criminal attorney):

"Well, let's look at it. Understand that this little girl had panties on. And then long underwear. Typical garb for a little girl going to bed. When they found her she has blood on her panties but not on the long underwear so this indicates to me that if there was a sexual assault somebody would have to redress this little girl. Which is bizarre behavior by a stranger who comes in and then commits this type of act and then would redress her, particularly if the pants were urine stained."

Cyril Wecht, MD (forensic pathologist/attorney who would later co-write a book on the JonBenet case and argue vociferously for a sexual motive in the murder including the embarrassing assertion that JonBenet died as a result of a bad game of sexual asphyxiation):

"May I remind you that previously released information tells us that there was blood on the labia, blood in the vaginal vault, an abrasion and contusion so we definitely have a sexual assault. The red staining on the panties, I'll bet you anything, is blood. And the question is how does it get there. It gets there from the blood on the

138

genitalia. And Mr. Silverman has correctly pointed out that there's no way that this could be done. The panties were placed back on to the child after the sexual assault had occurred in order for the staining to have been there in the crotch of the panties."

Cyril continues to get excited and, after the commercial break, talks clinically about inflammation and discoloration and the hymen and the rim and finally concedes that perhaps the rape of the child wasn't a vicious attack "maybe not by a penis" but rather was a "controlled situation".

D29. *This is how you become a creep. You need to fit all that hearsay and cheap information that you've collected and then jam it into the tiniest little box that you can handle called your Tastes. And then you have to hope just as desperately that the tragic little realities that you've tried to touch by simply constantly masturbating your mass onto your palm and belly are the true tragic realities of those who have already proved their tacky ability at selling, at low ball prices, all the reality that any loser like you would buy and care to believe.*

5. Hairstyle?

Geraldo does the same show as Rolanda, Maureen O'Boyle (*In Person*), Maury Povich, Jenny Jones, even *CNN Talk Back Live*. That is: trot the little girls who make up the small numbers of the little Miss Beauty Pageants and tut tut the perverse sexuality by ending with the murder and rape of its most famous representative.

Susan Rook of CNN asks one of the little assembled beauty queens all done up like a little executive rather than a Miss America: "Natasha; do you want to be a tomboy?"

The eleven-year-old little Miss Michigan replies through heavy lip gloss on big sexy lips:

"No, I don't. I want to be a little girl for as long as I can possibly be. Because I just want to live my childhood in pageantry isn't my whole life. I just want to be a little

girl."

Of course, Little Miss Michigan is already too old. The question should have been asked to one of the smaller younger made-up dollies that were dressed up as princesses.

D30. *The acts performed by Brooke Ashley don't change with extra information. Because they don't matter. 23-year-old Tricia and old man Marc fucking on film makes the same small sense as renting virtually any gay porn video anywhere at any price. Especially the newer ones that all include condoms and seriously careful wide open mouth cum shots. The possibilities and stories and fake concern for their own welfare and cottonmouthed regrets all show up in places very far away from the video monitor. Brooke crying. Brooke reading an article on Tricia Devereaux. Brooke listening to what Marc Wallace has to say personally over publicly. The air that swirls over her head with gossip and all those fanboys saying her name and disease over and over. The titles of her videos. The money she can still glom. The cheap wooden peep show booths that play any porn actress' video while some hard knee'd faggot fills his asshole with a brand new strain of HIV. The life she swam in and supported and now has to prop up what little's left so that it'll not come crashing down even harder on her single weakest character yet.*

6. What sort of face would she have?

8-year-old Brittany and 9-year-old Breanne are interviewed on *Extra* as former pageant mates of JonBenet.

"Where's JonBenet now?"

"She's up in heaven."

American Journal interviewed Breanne as well:

"It's kind of scary when I'm, like, far far away from my mom. Or my dad. It's kind of scary."

Breanne's mother, Dawn German, also contributed an article to *Newsweek* (January 20, 1997) as part of its cover story "The Strange World Of Jonbenet"; IT'S LIKE PLAYING DRESS-UP:

When she did her first swimsuit competition when she was 6, it was very age-appropriate. The suits were very cute, and they held beach balls.

Caryl And Marilyn (The Mommies) interviewed 11-year-old Dallas, 10-year-old Rebecca and 9-year-old Amy. Marilyn says Dallas looks like "Lolita" and that she had a "quick tense feeling" when they displayed such "sensual shots" of the tykes in full make-up.

D31. *A future Gang Bang Angels could just as easily be built around the Tawana Brawley fake rape case.*

Three or four or even more white men – some dressed in cop uniforms – take a young black porn starlet out into the woods and soak her in a cum bath after jamming two queer cocks into her cunt at the same time and making the nigger bitch take breathers at their assholes. They fuck her one after another in her naked pitch black asshole and when they're ready to ejaculate, they pull out and smear the sperm into her hair; already filthy with leaves and small sticks and dirt and mud.

Then a shaving scene where her nigger hair is cut clear of any evidence. Just before they make her crawl into a garbage bag. One of the voice-overs from one of the actor/rapists should be about how it feels to fuck the tight insides of four hundred years of oppression.

7. A pretty face?

Geraldo picks through a copy of *People* magazine that features JonBenet on its cover. He holds up a pageant program. And then, as images of JonBenet's swimsuited sex, lipstick and flirtatious bounces and grinds wash over him, he begins the real introduction:

"Found by her very own father, murdered brutally in the basement of her Boulder, Colorado home. Sexually assaulted before being strangled to death. But while the country watched the pictures of the little six-year-old on their televisions something else was also coming across. A powerful message. This was no ordinary girl who was murdered. This was a Pageant Queen. Even at the age of

six. Here she is in the first images the country had of the slain little girl. Doing apparently what she knew best: performing. Then there was this outfit. JonBenet in her pink cowgirl dress. Working the runway in front of onlookers. This black and white ensemble was next. Complete with matching top hat. Once again little JonBenet performing for points. For fame. But nothing brought forth the underlying story that was starting to disturb America like this still photo of JonBenet. Her hair styled perfectly. The bright red lipstick. All on a six-year-old child. What was this? What was this little girl involved in? And why were her parents doing this to her?"

Geraldo then admonishes the crowd to save their derision for the parents and not to treat the little children badly as they walk out onto the stage. He introduces each by name and comments on how charming each is in succession.

7-year-old Taylor.
"That's nice, I like your crown too."
8-year-old Brandy.
"Did your mom teach you that?"
8-year-old Tessa.
"Will you stand and show them your pretty dress? That's very lovely."
8-year-old Brooke.
"Can you show me that wave again?"
8-year-old Tabitha.
"Very nice."

D32. *The director may want to go that extra marketing distance for verisimilitude and sensationalist audiences by having the actors scrawl KKK and NIGGER NIGGER on her stomach and, unfortunately, big implant scarred tits. Then a shit-like substance over 80% of her body that'll show up the right shade on her dark shit-shade skin. He can always use a disclaimer about the need to tell the truth about the horrors of the crime and the effect that even the ideas have on one's repressed racist soul. He can broach the transgressive by seeking to investigate the polite limits of the public. Or the disturbing but undeniably erotic content*

of consensual and non-consensual rape fantasies. What better case to investigate truth and fantasy and power relations than one built from racist allegations in a sex case that most likely never happened.

There'll always be some low rung perverts that you can't worry about.

Better yet; The producers need to hire a black director. An old porn stud now put out to driving a bus or whatever. He'll do it.

He can expand on the details and outright deny the salacious references; all the while winking at his friends and employers and porn circuit audiences. He'll bask in outlaw artist status. He may want to simply suggest the humiliating denouement by having a male porn star smear his semen on the paid black whore's firm belly in what just may seem to look like the beginnings of a large K or something.

8. Would she be happy? Sad? What would her face be?

Jenny Jones reminded the audience who Jonbenet was. "Strangled and sexually assaulted" and then "she was gorgeous".

Of the mothers accompanying their pageant daughters, one had taken her daughter out of the circuit due to "too much pressure." This one, Donna, said her daughter Deidre had even competed against JonBenet. But now she was more realistic:

"My biggest fear is pornographic material. Any sleazy photographer can come in to these pageants, they will sell you videos of these pageants for $120. But they own the rights to those videos."

D33. *From Al Sharpton's autobiography; Go And Tell Pharaoh (Doubleday, 1996):*
On November 24, 1987, in the middle of the first Howard Beach trial, a fifteen-year-old black girl was found covered in racist graffiti and dog feces in a plastic garbage bag on the grounds of an apartment complex in

Wappinger's Falls, New York. The girl, Tawana Brawley, was rushed to the hospital and treated for trauma and sexual assault. Tawana told a story of having been abducted by a group of white men, held captive, and tormented, raped, and sodomized for several days.

9. What would her personality be?

JonBenet will be forever six years old – even though most of the photos of her are from when she was four and five. And she'll always have on either lipstick or duct tape wrapped around her little pouty unfittable mouth. Though there's certainly enough photos of her in the public feast being just a regular girl without make-up like something a paedophile wouldn't want to fuck over any other available child.

It is important to imagine that perhaps JonBenet was in fact molested before she was murdered. And while fiction is always ugly, the question of whether or not JonBenet, in later life, might have reacted negatively to the photos of her made-up like an adult looking to get paid or fucked does inform the photos I keep so carefully.

Could the little girls showing their legs and fannies and barely visible through diaper slits learn to see their innocent poses and struts and sliding holes as dirty. If I tell them I masturbate to them. If I show them. How I think of those red lips on such a little girl and imagine the brain numbing pain behind such tight bones. A bright red smudge on the head of my fat cock.

A paedophile who sits quietly as children play at the beach. A paedophile who just watches. And occasionally looks up from his book.

A finger that won't fit in. A cock that would cum only as he rubbed it along with her clumsily small palms and ignored directions. Her red suffocating face turning the lipstick you put all over her thin lips a brand new angry crumbling shade. The way her parents set her up for it wholesale. Delivered the pornography right into my lap for, what, $120.

D34. *The black actress would be paid better than her male co-stars. It would be a mistake for any black actress in the porn field to pass up the chance at such a juicy incendiary industry attention grabbing part.*

It would be an even better part for a new girl. Someone fresh. One that had certain reservations towards her chosen life and that maybe just wanted to test the water a little bit.

Because jobs are hard to get. Acting. And harder still for african-americans. And worse; women of color.

10. And would she be clean, tomboyish or dirty?

JonBenet is only known to me because she was murdered. And that death is all that lets me see the rape – desperately clung to despite the gross stupidity of perverts like Cyril Wecht – and all the bruises and sores and inflammations spread out onto bodies mostly older than her own and not exactly the same.

JonBenet is flat. As in the way a child of her age would be. No tits. Unformed. No fatty cunt and thighs and bags under her eyes and stretch marks. Soft and hard where there's nothing but skin on bone. Tired. Selfish. Bumps where saline will go soon enough. Tape here. Hide those. Exercise this more.

She is even flatter. As in paper. As in pathetic. As in pause and sound bite and used all by your lonesome self again and again.

And worse. I don't know any real facts and details about the little reproductions due to the intense self-serving speculations of even her most minute vital statistics. I know burly voices slick with muddy inference and salty with effeminate concern.

D35. *More from Al Sharpton:*
        I cannot describe the horror I felt upon hearing the full details of this story. No black person is without historical memory of the outrages visited upon black women throughout slavery and into the twentieth century. I was interested in this case because I felt someone had to

<u>stand up and defend this young girl; I felt like I was
defending my mother, my wife, my daughters, my sisters,
all the black women I know and love, black women in
general, even. Something had to be done.</u>

11. When you put a girl like that in the chair – picture the girl – what do you think when you see a girl like that?

I'm not telling you how hypocritical these detailers are. The same way I didn't give you the phone number to CHILDHELP USA to help you escape. But if that works for you and the various judges and prosecution and investigators who may be interested: Fine. You're welcome. Thank you.

Because I'm not the one to do it. The distant moral stance and thick condomed safety that separates those who talk about it in public and those who worry about it in private all seems to hinge on the very nineties hyper-concern for family and, specifically, the protection of children so that they can remain children for as long as they can. I don't have children – literally and figuratively – and I'm not so misanthropic to believe that all that adults say is somehow smarmy. The same way I don't believe that all good is done for the next generation.

But I'm clear on this. That this, from the *National Enquirer* of October 28, 1997, works best for those who masturbate into condoms thinking about Polly Klaas' pain, her father's mouth and her fully clothed ubiquitous image:

<u>Hoffmann-Pugh disclosed that JonBenet was
terribly embarrassed to be seen naked by anyone including
her daughter Ariana. 'If I happened to walk in on her and
she had her top off, she'd make a face and quickly fold
her arms over her chest and turn away from me', the
housekeeper recalled.</u>

<u>It was very clear that she was alarmed and didn't
want anyone seeing her chest, even though she was
completely undeveloped.</u>

D36. *Underneath the Gang Bang Tawana volume whatever*

title, in splashy white text, so as to leave no doubt in the
heads of stupid racist assholes that may want to
masturbate the wrong way to such images:
   "For all the black women I know and love, black
women in general, even."

12. What else do you think?

In the second photo of Emily, 10, in the photo book Fast
Forward (Growing Up In The Shadow Of Hollywood) by
Lauren Greenfield (Knopf, Melcher Media, 1997), the little
rich girl supermodel poses in the bathroom mirror of a
rather ritzy hotel. She's wearing the same hot pink
swimsuit that she wore in the previous photo but this time
it's dry. Her ass is pushed out, her long brown hair is held
back in a sexy flow, she looks as if she's starting to bud
breasts. But she's probably just a little too chubby. Her
pink lips don't look as pink or thick as they do in the shot
of her closing her eyes and dreaming in the pool. She says:
   In the bathroom, there are mirrors everywhere,
just like I love. It's kind of fun, because I can spend five
hours looking at myself in the mirror and doing my hair
and posing for myself. I want to be a model for magazines
and videos and TV shows and stuff.

D37. *From Unholy Alliances by Mike Taibbi and Anna Sims-*
Phillips (Harcourt Brace Jovanovich, 1989):
   According to the girl's aunt, Juanita Brawley,
Tawana was found dazed and confused Saturday
afternoon in a neighborhood where her family once had a
residence. Passers-by noticed her incoherent state and
brought her to St. Francis Hospital in Poughkeepsie. Upon
examining the young girl, doctors observed that her hair
had been chopped off, her body smeared with feces, and
the word KKK written in Magic Marker across her chest.
On her stomach, "nigger, nigger" was written. She had
been raped; her face bruised, body scratched. She was
treated for her injuries as well as shock and released to her
mother and aunt early this morning. The popular, attractive
cheerleader from Ketchum H.S. in Wappinger's Falls is so

shaken she is unable to speak.

13. What else do you think?

The Chicago Tribune on July 27, 1999, under the headline;
MICHIGAN POLICE HUNT MAN IN RAPE OF TWO GIRLS:
The man was wanted in the rape of two girls,
ages 8 and 14, who were found bruised and bleeding
Saturday in the farming community along Clio Area Bike
path, about 10 miles north of Flint.
The girls told authorities a man approached them
as they walked along the bike path and threatened them
with a knife.
He raped both girls, handcuffed one, then beat
and choked them until they lost consciousness, Genesee
County Sheriff Robert Pickell said.
"He may have thought they were dead. It appears
he wanted them dead", Pickell said.
Two days later the *Tribune* reported again. Under
MAN CHARGED IN SEXUAL ASSAULT OF 2 GIRLS:
Jack Duane Hall, 34, was arraigned in District
Court on charges of first-degree criminal assault with a
dangerous weapon and attempted murder by strangulation
in the attack on the 8- and 14-year-old girls, said Genesee
County Sheriff's Lt. Mike Rau.
Bleeding from where?

D38. *The actress should not speak. Over the opening
credits a group of happy sexy cheerleaders practising their
liberating youthful cheers should be filmed from behind
the chain link school fence.*

14. That's what the target is: she has a skirt on but no pants?

A primary use for child pornography is to lower children's
inhibitions. To show them shots of others doing what you
want them to do. This really isn't true often enough.
Put on this lipstick, dear. Just like mommy does.
Just like little JonBenet.

The Examiner of April 22, 1997:

Even before she was killed, bootlegged pictures of JonBenet and the innocent child's beauty pageant videos were a huge hit with sick paedophiles who spend hours glued to x-rated kiddie porn on the internet, say insiders.

The Star of April 29, 1997 (included under their JONBENET DAD LINKED TO KIDDIE PORN exposé):

Girls who appear as young as 10 or 12 engaging in sexual acts – including oral sex – with each other and with men.

Pre-teen girls, bound and gagged, being whipped and tortured.

A girl of no more than 12 or 13 bound from her head to her hips in a leather bridle, and hung by a chain. In the full-color photo, she is made to appear dead.

D39. *The porn company, frightened by possible lawsuits and costly legal entanglements, may think it best to choose a different name for the Tawana character just like it would have to choose an older age. Juanita, after Tawana's media hungry aunt, might be an ironic and powerful choice.*

From Unholy Alliances:

Juanita: "She had feces smeared all over her, in her hair. Her pants were burned. Um, she was incoherent. I saw "KKK" scrawled on her, written on her chest, right over her breasts. Further down there was "nigger nigger" written on her stomach."

15. What are you wanting to do with her and to her?

It's not a mouth I fucked. Not a small available body that I beat up just to do what her fucking father did. I wasn't that drunk and stupid and repressed.

Her mother didn't ask me to do it to her. By putting make-up on her and asking her to walk the way she used to when she was slightly older and more knowledgeable and far more trained in the ways of courting and selling and giving it up to the wrong loser time and time again.

I didn't pick the target. I don't have to take the one that old cunt chose for all the other idiots.

D40. *The end credits should scroll over long slow motion pans of project houses and crack corners. And at the very end, just before the behind the scenes make-up and new age complicity footage, the legend, once again, from the box-cover about how all this has been done for the black women the director and all the other care givers see as voiceless and in need. Long freeze frame to fade. Then back up to lighten the mood with actor details and motivation.*

16. But what would you want to do with her if she was in this room now? You're on your own with her: what would you be thinking about? What would you like to do?

I wouldn't put make-up on her. I'd leave it on, though, if she came that way.

You know how many times I've heard those stories about how child molesting fathers didn't have to ask their children for their bodies after a while. That the kids would become trained soon enough. And if they found themselves alone in the house with their dad they'd usually just strip off and go for daddy's dick as he just sat there. She'd pull him into the bedroom. Just little children.

That's what I would be thinking. That's what I'd like to do. To see how that comes up from the first time you nail her little face and tiny hands and stretch her child's vulva to adult coming shreds. To watch that coming up like vomit. Under the tears and the running mommy make-up. Underneath her dress and trailer trash t-shirts and tight swimming trunks and peanut butter breath.

Now. I'd look for specifics.

D41. *Truth is I wouldn't look for porno stars' names or titles if it weren't for such information. And I know I can't see the infection rate physically go up when some dick pulls off and dumps his perfectly clean DNA'd cum directly*

into some cheap cunt's gaping asshole. I'm sold all the information and I buy it up. She got HIV at someone's house while fucking another porn star for athletic fun and drugs. She was just that way. And she was ugliest when it was just her acting that was bad and her used female stupidity couldn't not seep through. It was the low level she started at and the way she denied it as she slid further down. The tears and the trembling and mild composure fits are only as good as her awareness of the cameraman and her professional relative ease at selling absolutely any part of her that's asked for.

17. Right. Where?

I'd tell her she wasn't lying. That I knew she was more than just a piece of junk. And my problem with her make-up was just that: My problem.

And I'd explain about her father. How ignorant he is and how she deserves so much better and how, still, she'll always be better than what he's trying to make her.

And that she should feel pretty. Because she is. And not in a dirty way. Not in some ridiculous romantic way. Not in a bullshit way. She would be pretty all her life because she had something special to offer the world. In the way she'll carry herself and be above all of this filthy weak shit and in the way she'll be able to cut through all the lies and phoniness and manipulations that people – scum – that want to tear her down and deplete her will try and use against her.

I'd like to hug her if she wants me to.

If she asks me.

I'd like her to know she's safe with me. That she should feel protected, at least, sometimes. That she owes that to herself. That the world owes that to her, correct, but she can't always count on it.

Let me see the scars. The cuts and bruises. Let me see the future snack shop waitress underneath all that make-up and let me explain pornography to her. You don't need it. Unless you want it. I'd ask her. Make up your own mind.

Where do you fit here? Where?

JonBenet was a six-year-old beauty brat who smeared her dead raped body all over my reading material and television and masturbation fantasies. You don't want that, do you?

And I'd feel the pulse in my cock.

And I'd want to tell her what the physical manifestation of love is supposed to be. I'd show her everything. Before she was ready.

D42. *How many women have had pool sticks jammed up their freshly raped and ripped wombs and then been cracked over their heads with the blood splattered broken wood ends. Had their faces and bodies beaten into bleeding pulp by angry drunk bar patrons showing off for their buddies, after their cocks have gone limp inside the sloppy fifths of the passed out still fuckable corpse. How many nigger whores were ever concerned that they might have contracted AIDS through an overly aggressive john's mouth fucking. How many have had to abort john's or pimp's children and then been collegiate nurse lectured about the incredible dangers of unprotected sex as they soaked their sore pits and glands in orange juice and cookies. How many went and fixed that very same night, had a bump before they got home and fucked the same exact sort of man again and again before they allowed themselves even a little nap between nods and faints.*

18. What's the word for those?

What did mommy teach you?

Did you ever ask: What are you covering up. What's getting hid. And all these lies about honesty and how important that is to a little girl thrashing around in the dark. And a haggard mother trying far too hard. And a horny fat masturbating faggot face fucker. Ask: How deep do you push to hit honesty?

Truth.

You don't look for truth, asshole, you swim in it. The cum on your knuckles and the tell-all stains on the

crotch of your jeans and the burning blisters on the shaft of your cock are all due to what some little piglet does every day from then on for the rest of her life. How fucking stupid can you be? How pathetic.

Soul. Spirit.

It's impossible to not talk about the souls in pornography. From the teenagers who choose to lift their shirts in drunken youthful liberation to the hard over-worked bodies of pop porn starlets modelled as come-uppance for Hollywood stereotypes all the way down to the wilfully reckless misfits who accept candied degradation and outright humiliation as laughing nigger-rich answers to bright and certain futures. These women – mainly women – believe and operate only under the belief that an inner protecting wonder separates themselves from their acts. Or, more contemporaneously popular, that the big deep extra is being fed and celebrated. Even.

They're still miles above – far away – from the dirty little worlds that sad fucking lonely monsters like me cling to.

And a mature woman tells me she wouldn't make the same mistakes the immature one did and now she would try harder to not miss out on all the fun she could have had if she were looser and less stuck-up; less frightened.

There's so much to learn she says.

Education.

The be-all and end-all of one's sex life shouldn't be continuously spent alone. So says the common denominator. So you take all the porno boxes displayed on all the many walls of the second floor of Nationwide Video and you compare the face of these plugged holes to the only plugged once face of little six-year-old JonBenet Ramsey and you look as hard as you can for the one that'll take you away from all of that.

And you rent it.

You compare her to the poses and the press and smiles and morals and the wholesaling and the adjectives of the backless mob telling you what they can sell you under the strict US government guidelines and beat off, at

home, to second best.

You owe it to yourself.

And the skinny faggot who takes you to his stinking like sickness apartment, who only requires that you buy him a six pack of cheap beer or two on the way up asks you if you want him to wear one of his outfits for you. Because he knows who you are. And he asks you to call him JonBenet. If you like. For him too. As he places his lipsticked wet mouth on your stiff cock and drags his stained and thrushed tongue up your ass and across your balls. And into your mouth. Making everything he smears pink.

Because it's different when you're naked and in bed, dear, because you can't lie as easy and it demands a greater sense of commitment. It's too much work to always hide. Too much work to never give in.

D43. *How many nigger whores have sucked on the dicks of men whose last few hours had been spent at faggot peep booths. The stink of men who beer belch and lap at the hairy sacs of other men mixing with the slimy latex and chemical smell of the prophylactic on the flat of their tongues. The mouth stick of sick young men and sloppy old dirty men greasing up hard in her palm as she tries to cheat a bit before her jaw does the hard but safe work. So few johns must wash. So few johns leave their homes to go fuck the insides of niggers. These horny animals waste time by eating other men on their lunch hours and in the middle of their drives to and from work. And what do the hookers care? Even if the crack and smack didn't cancel out the wretched mud acts and disgusting wants and requests and all the cheaper and cheaper demands, then certainly the sheer boredom of men turning deep into men would. Just the same. It's the wives and girlfriends and dates and friends that care. The ones that want it clean. Who are stupid enough to think it matters. That there's some self-respect there. Some comfort. Something worth something more. Good girls.*

19. What is the clinical word?

"Luck" works.
  "De minimus" does as well.

D44. *How much to fuck you in the ass?*
  How much do you want?

Answers 1–41 from pages 93–96 of SEX, edited by Boyd McDonald, Gay Sunshine Press, San Francisco, 1982. Questions (G42) 1–6 from THE TRIAL OF IAN BRADY AND MYRA HINDLEY, edited by Jonathan Goodman, David Charles, Devon, 1973. Questions (G46) 1–7 from pages 201 and 202 of MALE INTERGENERATIONAL INTIMACY, edited by Theo Sandfort, Edward Brongersma & Alex van Naerssen, Harrington Park Press, New York, 1991. Questions (G47) 1–15 from pages 10 and 11 of THE CHILD LOVERS, Glenn D. Wilson & David N. Cox, Peter Owen, London, 1983.

1. 15 in their late teens or early 20s. Had to stop after rain started in the wood of a country club.

Another english Lesley; this one a year older but with a mental age of only six. Already so different than our dear sweet bright Lesley.

From *Innocents* by Jonathan Ross with Steve Panter and Trevor Wilkinson (Fourth Estate 1997):

The forensic scientists and pathologists would soon confirm that, mercifully, she had not been sexually abused, but that, although she had not been interfered with, her last companion had undoubtedly obtained some sexual pleasure from her final hours on earth.

I remember what the little pig wore when she was missing and how it changed when she was found. Soaked in blood and hard mud and spotted with old cum. Different from the photos I have of her, aged ten, squinty eyes like a play ragged moppet. Different from the pictures I used to keep of little dutch rats getting fucked as they pretend to half-sleep. Different, still, from the drawings Trevor Brown did in high contrast black and white of little girls with bugs and guns and their harsh lily white legs spread open, their skinny uncomfortable mouths filled with whatever Mr. Brown put in there right then. But I make them all the same.

It is known only that the killer had masturbated onto Lesley, and that he had killed her, brutally, stabbing her twelve times in the chest and neck with a small knife, before wiping the blade on her thigh and leaving her, uncovered, to the elements.

Oh dear god, let her be safe.

She wore a blue coat with a fake fur hood. And under that, over her easily guarded pre-teen pre-human female damage, keeping her safe and entertained and distracted, was a pink skirt, a white t-shirt and these charming tartan socks featuring the name of her favorite 1975 pop group: Bay City Rollers.

Upon her underwear forensic scientists were to find semen, but whether the man had ejaculated in some private, quiet place, or up in the winds and mists of the

moors, whether he had done so when she was alive or dead, would also remain unknown.

E. ARE YOU SEXUAL WITH CHILDREN?

E1. *No.*

2. Most were. A very few were dirty or had a strong smell.

This is pretty close to perfect. All you do is look. And masturbate. And fuel and twist. Clarify. Seethe. Hide.

And it's more than simple self-control. Isn't it? Like art. Like love. Like getting high. Like screaming at some poor bereft mother about how you particularly like fucking this one photo of her daughter over and over again. Just as you'd imagine the crack head who split her tiny project frame all open did. Thank you. You mutter when you're done. It's like living with it. All the time.

You wanna know what a cheap motherfucker is? You wanna know the best way to do it? You want to get as close as you can without – sticking it in, getting any on you, getting caught, putting it in your mouth?

The worst thing an artist can do is perform for an audience. To create something for an effect. To look for a response to justify his neotonous obsessions and confusion and think that the exercise is legitimate due to some misunderstood lazy form of shock or compliance.

No one would believe it anyway.

E2. *I'm told I hurt children. I don't really believe it. I'd like to be convinced. If for no other reason than it would make my petty deviousness and misplacements seem more legitimate; less desperate or paranoid. More worthwhile. As it is, it all looks rather pathetic. Silly. Ugly. Frightened and angry and lonely. Like someone who's compelled to search for sex even though he disdains it. Who's come to hate it because of a need that he can't fulfil or explain. Rather than hating it for its own lack. Of course, that resentment must lead to him creeping around between*

safety and stupidity; between vivid fantasies and clumsy
violence. With contorted grasping reality in the middle.
Mixing and confusing sex with pornography. Twisting
unrequited inversions.

3. Very few had cum I didn't like.

I cut out newspaper photos of all these special little girls.
It's almost always little girls. There's more girls than boys.
And I put the paper bits onto xerox machines and I enlarge
the images. The paper is bright white underneath the face
that turns from cheap newspaper grey into harsh black
dots. There are no small details. The image becomes
general and flat and whole. The idea becomes intentional. I
keep these at home and use them as pornography. I can
no longer find any commercial pornography worthwhile.

I jam the clipped photos into my pockets. I want
them to tear and flake and disintegrate. They are not
precious. They are dirt. Garbage. They are used cheap
newsprint that costs no more than the entire newspaper at
no more than fifty cents a day. This is all very small. Very
little. Unimportant. They don't even adequately represent
the lies that families and friends continue to mouth even
after the now missed thinglet is buried. Anymore. Children
are convenient. For their parents. The shots of their
children's faces are grey and flat and sold.

I want to believe that the work I put into these
smiling shots is genuine. Deserved. Honest. Natural glee –
taken at happy times that apparently need
commemorating. Times that were safe and paraded and
full of the promise badly planned but ostentatiously hoped
for. Tight. That love; that unique bond that is inexplicable
to those of us who don't pass our cum into bodies worthy
of reproducing and raising and worrying and protecting
and selflessly giving and sneaking off every small once in a
while.

The shots – the ones I picked that day when I
knew where I'd end up sooner or later – stay in my
pockets until after I cum in public. Then they end up on
the floor stamped on and unrecognizable, left to crumble

and soak their ink and grainy thin paper into the puddles of dead runny cum and shit smears and piss drops and steam and crabs and sperm feeding flies and lazy glossy black paint on cracked concrete.

I've seen men get on their hands and knees and lick at the cum and shoe sole filth left on the never swept floor. I've had a beast wipe my dripping cock with a kleenex that crumpled into small white fisted wet clumps that left white fuzz all over my mouth drenched crotch and then, like a retard, like a degenerate faggot, push the sticky wet tissue globs into his mouth, lick, bite and chew. All the while staring at me and masturbating his long hard angry cock.

This is something you do alone.

This is not a ritual.

I don't usually cum into napkins. I don't usually clean up. I shake drops that don't shoot into drool that covers and dissipates into hands and onto pants and shirts and strangers' fleshy asses and throats and chins and beards and docked hard cocks.

I leave the pictures in filth because that's where they belong but I don't feel that I'm returning them to their rightful place. I am uncomfortable calling them they. They mean so little to me everyday. Just like sex. And they take up so much of my time.

I mark and draw on the pictures. I cut them in pieces like raw kleenex nothings with a paperclip. I gouge at the little girls' faces and leave scratches in the table underneath. I bend the paperclips into long jagged spears and stick it through the photos into the wooden partitions in peep show back rooms. I leave the little dead raped rats hanging for other mouth hungry PC faggots who don't think about what they're doing. The suburbanite husbands find that they've sunk even lower. And worry more about the kind of cock they're getting stuffed on. The proprietors of these places don't say one fucking word to me. Because they don't care. About stupid assholes and their camp fucked kinks. Whatever. And I know this.

This is cheap. And ugly. Gross. Pathetic. And less than nothing to me. Shit. Garbage. Small. Fat. Sweaty.

Dark.

It's not humiliating. Though it should be. If all the lies that droop out of these mothers' and fathers' now supposed empty lives – lifes – had even the smallest root in reality. These thieves that care about whether or not I'm masturbating and staining and coveting their little birth breaths into my low sleazing belly mulching existence.

I want to fuck her kid. I want to fuck her little less child because it is her child. I want to fuck it because it will make its crying so much more personal. Harder. I don't want to fuck it like some seething faggot with a face full of ten cocks a night licking up the grease off the edges and flats from glory holes and beating his dog meat hard-on because he finally, desperately, needs to cum. I fuck it because it already hurts as quiet as it can.

E3. *There's an intense set of rules permeating every reported case of child sexual abuse. A fear of the law spread among universal morals hangs just above every single news head, simpering comforted confessional and well compensated world mother. I can't help but slither in context.*

4. Yes, I only found very few with cock cheese that I could enjoy.

Some of these girls are so tiny. Stomachs as flat as only growing baby fat allows. Faces so compact and lips too tight for two fingers.

I'm no more bored with sex than any of these other types: these fucking nigger drug addicts, husbands and fathers, and the ones that have to create jewelry for their genitalia or tattoos for their backs and trimmed pubics and positive mind expansion exercise excuses and temporary primitive fantasies. You don't need it. You don't need to make it interesting again. You don't need something that you just can't figure out quite yet. You don't answer for it. You want it. And you do what others want you to do. You just don't admit it. Even though you're so fucking used to it you've replaced why you

started with what the fuck were you doing. Why you keep hoping for more. Performing. Treading. It's as natural as VD. As phony as respect. And as warm and comforting as grease.

He wasn't going to leave first. Which is usually the case. I tucked myself back in and leaned into his pigging pretentious face:

"Swallow it."

I grabbed his balls underneath his slippery fist and cock action and squeezed tight. His faggot hand dropped and I took on my own slow rhythm. He chewed faster. Sloppier and slower and louder. Not because he was threatened. But because he sensed more sex. His eyes dropped. His concentration took over. The sweat in the booth, a new acceptance on his hard dick, a stranger's cum on cotton in his mouth – against his back teeth and down his tasting throat.

He came quickly. I pushed his cock up hard so that his sickening fourth cum of the day jism barely pulsed onto his hairy exposed stomach and shirt tails. One hand cupped his balls, the other shielded his cock. His sperm splashed onto my arm and wrist and soaked back around my palm.

"Swallow. Atta boy. Swallow it."

I didn't have a kleenex. I reached into my front pocket. His cum probably smearing along the inside seams and my keys and bucket change. My pants still unfastened around my cock, only kept up by the button at my waist. I felt my stink and his and pinched the photo of little Lesley Molseed that I kept nearest to my balls. The photo slice of murdered near-retarded Lesley and her mom's memory after her short eleven years of lessons and candy giggles and embarrassment dabbing up and wilting the pervert cum of this troll's long extended balmed gummed cock. I wadded the photo into my palm and used it to cup the pig's glans. I hoped he'd get a paper cut or a skin scratch nearest his piss hole. But the paper was too thin and cheap and wet and old. I hoped Lesley would turn to black blotches in his ill white running filth. I stroked back down the shaft, my careful skin protected from his slick tender

skin by Lesley as prophylactic dam. I tugged at his perpetually full balls. Lesley's big ugly english teeth biting at his sac. And pushed my fist and her wetted face farthest in, above the scumbag's bunched up pants, into his perineum and as close as I could get to his sweat soaked black asshole. Where I left it.

E4. *America's Most Wanted broadcast some footage of the film taken by Adrian Rosales with his very necessary camcorder. Of the nine and ten-year-olds he used to film at neighborhood kiddie pools and playgrounds. He planned on molesting them. And made a single botched attempt at a hotel. Which was why he was featured on that particular TV show – with the host that continues to suffer through the tragedy of having his son raped and murdered; who appears alongside Polly Klaas' father on so many other safety obsessed TV shows when the discussion for children in sexual danger seems, once again, appropriate. I can't see this material in any other context. It's all carefully and loudly framed for me. Regardless of my personal taste. Even the most cloistered and imaginary interests become predatory and dangerous. My sight becomes my sickness.*

5. Had a few rejections and insults, hit once, bitten once. Apt. robbed once and caught by vice cop I put the touch on, but I went to court and won.

I'm not the only one. I masturbate at home. Seeing this bastard's standing cock and seeping asshole and his thick mental disease when I use Lesley Molseed's new photo around my own.

This is what creates a creep. This is what creates art.

I look at the paintings of Trevor Brown. The way they are perfectly rendered to get as close to the real image as is possible by craft. And I know he does the same thing. I see the stand in. Not mere proxy for some juvenile sense of attack or greater violence involving the law and some mess and some very extreme and ugly degree of corporeality. But as use. To get as close as possible to what

that little dead girl means right now. Right then.

E5. *Alone in a room with such a pretty little child. I hugged her and felt her close against my crotch all bunched up and rough in jeans pushed against her moldable flesh and that tiny openable warm squealing hole and big eyes.*

6. Rest rooms of mews, theatres, parks, rest areas, shopping malls. The rest at my apt. and a good many in the car.

Trevor Brown from various issues of his mail order magazine *Taboo*:

I have no bad conscience about the use of small girls in my artwork – I'm not painting "Kiddie Porno". Child pornography has one blatantly obvious sexual intention – what I'm doing has much wider objectives – I suspect it's highly unlikely that sick paedophiles would find much to get off in my work.

As for personal taste, ie. for porn to actually do what it's intended to do, I have to find the girl real cute, the actual activity not that important. So, as under this criteria most Western pornography fails, I feed off the tacky images, grotesque close-ups, tastelessness, degradation, extreme perversions and, perhaps, most artistically stimulating of all, the glib smiles?

A shame that the majority of porno is so dull/ uninventive ...just following the set formula ...the primary intent is purely making vast amounts of money. Is there no one making porno for art?

I think of the bruises, etc. more as an enhancement emphasizing female fragility and beauty, suggestive of sexuality, rather than having a direct connection with violence. Perhaps it can be taken as a kind of surreal post-rape fantasy.

The real reasons for drawing young girls were more instinctive and 'innocent' though – as I said, it was mostly just a natural progression from drawing dolls and the interest in exploring the 'sinister innocence' theme. Plus, of course, I am living in Japan – the 'empire of cute' –

where such imagery is fairly commonplace and free of the over-reactionary nonsense going on in the Western World.

I've fetishized/sexualized bruises etc. to such an extent I can barely connect them with the cause– ...so if someone says my work is about violence I'm confused and saying 'Where? Where?' I can't see it.

No – I think of it more as an enhancement – emphasizing female fragility – like seeing a girl crying you want to wrap your arms around her and comfort her – ...but there is also an underlying sadistic appeal.

E6. *I put my finger straight in, all the way in.*

7. Usually all drop their pants, and I can feel their lovely ass.

There is a brief pause in the BBC documentary *Fear Of God: The Making Of The Exorcist* where, while director William Friedkin is basking in his genius, the camera is allowed to just barely pass over two still photos of twelve-year-old actress Linda Blair in perfect Hollywood make-up. Her face made to look deeply slashed by fresh bleeding scars down her slightly chubby cheeks, across her nose and into her soft redder lips. Looking very still. Emotionless. Her eyes naturally wide. As she waits for the test shots to be taken and evaluated.

William Friedkin: "One day I had this thought that the disfiguration that was ...that results in her face should come from something that Regan did to herself. And I thought what if – in the scene where she was masturbating with a crucifix we see that her whole face is streaming with blood. Fresh blood. As though she had used the crucifix to scar herself."

Friedkin's hands claw down his face as he speaks to bring the point home.

Miserable perverts can rewind back to the shots and freeze. Linda Blair the actress. Linda the child. The parents and their contracts. The simulated vicious sex acts and the foul sex spat language and the immediate and cumulative effects on shocking unprotected pre-teen

purity. The character and its simple puzzle parts that seem to mean more to all the other well paid industry interviewees even though all their answers about such are couched in high moral social concern about the little girl under the make-up. Under the pulleys and lights and straps and instructions. Linda explains that she didn't learn that she was meant to look like she was masturbating until years later. And that her prosthetic tongue jabbing is horrible to look at.

E7. *So perhaps the answer is Yes. But I know the answer is as ridiculous as the question. Which is where I operate. Where I stay on the hamster wheel.*

8. I used to always want to be sucked off, but now not so much because of the high rate of VD.

A young girl pisses into a urinal almost as tall as she is. Her panties down around her thighs stopped by her stretched down black fetish stockings.

Trevor Brown paints carefully articulated bruises on the perfect sexual spots – under the thighs and down the legs and small nicks on the small breasts. He knows to tie her arms back. A lipstick smear that careens back towards an asian ear is a convincing and extremely personal gesture.

He delicately touches tiny brown nipples and clear running tears and twists the bandages and smiles and stains and confusion into plastic toy dolls. Which makes sense when you consider what it takes to draw and imagine and follow through and airbrush these acts before displaying them.

I see that extreme need in Balthus and Darger. In Helnwein and Klossowski. And every single one denies it. I don't see it in Mann and Araki and Hamilton or Sturgis. Unless I want to. Every now and again. Like Lewis Carroll and Mary Ellen Mark's beauty queens. Like Dorthea Lange's Damaged Child. There's a craft that some feel the need to master and wildly perform within its wide open parameters simply because the craft exists. Like a

166

songwriter trying to write a perfect song. And then there's the others for whom the craft is purely indulgent.

It's just that easy to turn the best intentions into child pornography. Rather like parenting. One would assume.

It's all in the seeing where the crucifix would slice and how the hot blood would drip and stream. How deep you need the new scars to be. And knowing that you need to see it.

F. DO YOU HATE WOMEN BECAUSE YOU CAN'T FUCK CHILDREN?

F1. *A question I prefer. Because it contains "Fuck" and "Children" and "Women". I like the way someone specific would choose the ideas and string them all together. It seems so perfect. And my answer should be as equally sexual. And still proclaim, in as slippery a voice as possible: No.*

9. At one time three times a week, but now usually only once or twice a week.

How many nigger whores have sucked on dicks belonging to men whose last few hours had been spent on backroom knee crawls. The nigger's coffee belches are worse. But. The same brand of stomach churning swallows rising up through tired tongues and hurt gums. An unwashed bite. A latex tang. Barely edible spew from over-worked, over-tasted, over-wet flesh. The fast food approach to digestion and disease. And the hard truth that the john, even with his money still in loose change, knows full fucking well that what the hooker does is so much more terrible than what he does. And so much more hideous because of that. The way she's let herself steamroller over her african-american self.

I stuck two fingers through a glory hole and jabbed straight into a flabby fatty sticky ass. The death pit on the other side pushed harder against the partition and started to position his slack doughy flesh up hole to hole.

He waited and groaned and wriggled as I fingerfucked his soft shit stench until I could get hard enough to slip my cock all the way inside him. Nigger whores watch you. I replaced my slick stinking fingers with a slipping loose fuck and cummed inside his kneading gutting corpse. Again.

F2. *Brooke Ashley turns up in the very first American Bukkake video. She with her HIV history made public. She keeps a champagne glass tucked tightly under her chin to catch all the cum that might hit that rather than her ethnic face. The same one you can rent. To see it cry about turning HIV. Or collecting thick sold loads before she even knew. Maybe while she got it.*

10. I was staying overnight with my cousin and he said, look over here. He was jerking off, so I did it. I was 12 then. Me, a cousin & a stepbrother were just playing around and got into sucking each other, and then I told a friend and we did it; then there was this 13-year-old boy on my paper route who I talked into it, and I was well on my way, but really came out in the Air Force. I went in at 16 for 6 mos. At first I spit it out but then tried it one time and liked it.

A boy I used to go to school with showed me how to have sex in the restrooms whenever time even slightly started to drag. I'd sit on the toilet with my pants down around my ankles. He'd suck me off a little to get me wet and then spit into his fingers to do the same to his asshole. Then he'd put his feet on my knees and sit flush down on my cock while I leaned back as far as I could into the tank behind me. So I could pump in as far up his tight faggot asshole as my arms and thighs could steady. His pants and shoes and, after a while, the women's satin panties he'd taken to wearing would be placed carefully on the tank to keep the metal and porcelain from banging too loudly.

I'd cum straight up into his ass somewhat quickly and painfully and he'd often try to jab his hard-on down onto my balls and thighs. As much as he could. The smell of his shit and my cum was sometimes overwhelming. And

we'd carry the stench out with us into the rest of class.

If I was feeling more aggressive and a lot more reckless, I'd just sit him down on the toilet and fuck his face. I'd cum into his mouth and piss and turn around to get my asshole rimmed while I beat myself off so we could start again.

He'd stare at a nude model during certain figure drawing classes and I knew – no matter how homely or little dicked or female the model was that day – that I'd end up cumming into one of his bored mindless holes before lunch break.

F3. *This could be payment. This could be payback. The corralled strangers dump their filth on her because she has been rendered worthless and, worse, dangerous to the collective biology. She represents the rat teeth of infection through human need. Or is she simply wretched because of her laziness and ignorance. Or her ready willingness to exploit what little she has left so bottom shelf cheaply.*

She is still there. To re-infect. By her own design. Her own seething sense of vigilante revenge. Like a John Walsh hunting for all the child molesters like the one that cut his son's darling little baseball cap'd head off. And getting paid for it. Just like this one. On her knees. With her mouth open. Licking at the spewed cum and bristling against the violently pumping hard hands working to bring about the personal private act of self-orgasm. She wants to bring it on. A compensated tool. A funnel. A symbolic humiliation. An easy job. Cum here. Right there. And do it yourself, just thinking and looking. Just aiming. And she adapts that subservient position lower than the fat, bloated, animalizing congealed mass of male and sticks her tongue out like she does when she gets checked for thrush and mimes: Fine. Put it here. Look at this. Pay me. Sucker. Sucker. Suckers.

11. I mainly sit down over a cup of coffee and talk them out with hinting to see how they respond, then I'll invite them to my apt. – that is, if they are not negative to the hints.

A mexican glory hole queen who insisted on showing me his soft pink stained panties asked me to please cum in his ass when I was done with his mouth and ready to shoot. It belongs in my ass, he kept telling me, as he licked and bit at the tight white condom I insisted on wearing.

F4. *You have to take her into her mother's bedroom and sit her down on the marital bed. You show her what she has to look forward to. You appeal to her vanity.*

You start to tweeze at her tiny thin girly eyebrows. Pluck every single gentle hair out of her tight furrowed strained forehead. Keep her quieter. Yank each single small hair out one at a time. Explain why you have to do this. So that she'll become pretty.

12. This school is more a youth jail, so they have as much to lose as I do. Also, when the boys get mad they call just about everybody fag, so no one pays attention to it. They don't want the mess any more than I do. One has to know how to cover his ass.

"I can't go in some of these places anymore. I've been yelled at before and others, I suspect, just have to remember me. And, after you're defiled enough, you don't want to go in there anymore anyways.

I kept leaving spent full soaked condoms on top of the coin boxes. Sometimes I'd drain the cum out onto the coin slots and slap the sticky fused condom across the video screen.

Some of these other skanks leave their shit smeared all over the walls and screens."

F5. *Tell her: She has a choice. That there is no real difference between an earth mother bagged down with lumpy hips and facial hair and pure goddess stupidity and then a plastic'd shiny face teetering like wax above big fat tit implants and youthful hard gym obsessions. That it's mom's job. Not yours. And although you have nothing extra special to bequeath, you still haven't met one single brand of spread waitress that was actually worth a fuck.*

13. I'd say 90 percent and 5 percent will go bisex. The other 4 will be gay.

You pull the weakest one out. The sheep don't want it and it's the easiest one to do.

Women and children first. Absolutely.

I've started to fetishize the lack of choice.

F6. *That you haven't ever seen or met a stripper who really was above her station. Just like a mom who didn't need make-up.*

14. Yes.

How many faggots have told me about their lovers dying. How many fag creeps have handed me condoms as they've lowered themselves to my crotch just to show me they care what I just might think of them and their personalities.

F7. *Explain about battered wife syndrome and how fawning manipulations work well with fissure insecurities. Tell her to go get her little brother and see if he would put up with all of this.*

Tell him to strip next to his sister. Tell them both to look. Tell them both to kiss. Make sure the sister has enough lipstick put on her puffy little child lips to smear the excess onto the boy's own harmless culpability.

See that his little penis becomes stained in bright pink sister. And that it rises and thickens against his fear and surprise. And that he reaches across to pinch her mosquito bite sized nipples on her flat boney chest just like faggots do. Don't be gentle; tell him. Look at her forehead. Underneath the red raw plucks and tiny specks of blood. She shouldn't fucking look like that. She won't ever look any better now. Not without the appropriate shadow and concealment lessons.

15. Jockey shorts.

Before he goes out slobbing and stuffing, he's taken to drinking big glasses of milk and eating big bowls of sugared cereal drenched in even more milk. To make his piss more fluorescent. To make it taste like JonBenet's.

F8. *You shouldn't confuse what you're doing with what you're watching. Laws do that. And psychologists who are paid by the hour, just like the judges and attorneys and police officers and TV talk show crews, don't want to explain the difference away too neatly.*

What I'm thinking has to stay perfectly clear. I know how safe and removed and perfect in mind these truths are. There's nothing to be gained by making reality a fantasy.

Six-year-old Kayla McKeen was sent to school with make-up on her little blonde face. Her father, and possibly her mother, were trying to hide the black eyes and bruises she had.

16. Yes.

You can't go home with people for sex. Dirt becomes mud if you wait too long. Your fingers smell like their shit reached out from sweat pooled assholes and unhealthy stomachs and irresponsible brains.

"Why do you want me to make you sick?"
And:
"This doesn't get any better."
It's a simple mistake of age. An ugly mistake that, as difficult as it is to live through at the time, will only get worse as you're forever forced to reconsider the urge over the act while you slowly sober up.

His asshole in your face and your digging shit thick fingers and shit smeared knuckles and shit stained forearms and all the bends and grunts and growls and liquor soaked need to get in deeper and deeper until you pass out with the hot mess on your chest and wrinkled dick and collapsed balls amid the hot morning flies and kitchen roaches.

"You should insist on a condom, really – it's for

you as much as me."

You came in his throat yesterday. Today it's necessary that you deposit directly into his intestines and, because you're just that drunk enough to be polite, somehow you'll make sure that he'll cum. But, as he needs to play the Nell this short tired life, it is not acceptable for you to slink into any of the real work.

Twice is like boyfriends. Except he knows your reputation. And if you were nice at all, it'd blow the cheap cartoon fantasy for him and his faggy peers. Which is why you're getting laid. Otherwise; if you treated him even half-human, you'd discover that this skinny little young faggot with make-up all over his fuck face and your cock wouldn't touch any bit of you, or anyone else similarly unaffected. He didn't buy or steal all that make-up just to get what all the other cunts can get.

You make him clean your fingers. That shouldn't have been in him if it weren't for his lap dog tongue.

Your hand went there to see how far his yapping corpse stretched and how black and stubborn his pit sank. Till he started bleeding infection and toxins inside that widened hurting damaged hole. All the time fighting through the liquor to see if you could feel his sloppy lazy face on your sac and glans and shaft without actually watching it. You stayed hard because of the old smell of friendly shit on medicinal fish gas and the cold on wet face and fist clawing and pumping.

"You filthy faggot" slurred into that dead father's hole that you tried – a couple of times now – to spit into rather than lovingly rim. Faggots search with their tongue. Girls are used to the taste of warm fresh dirty shit.

He got his small face punched. Hard. Drunk. When he asked for a little violence. To make the palsied common variety fucking he was slithering on just a little harder, just a little rougher and just a little closer to the ugly death he always figures he deserves for spreading his womanly asshole like this. He got his full shaved balls yanked and his veiny neck choked; his skinny blotchy pale back scratched and slapped and his hair towelled off a good amount of his own shit.

He cried. Like one of Trevor Brown's streaming little girls. And both of you stopped flat when you came into his ass; his long dog cock standing straight up and bouncing everywhere but into his palms that held him tight onto the couch. He had maybe hoped to finish himself off at the same time, or to protect his made-up greasy face from the sting of more hated slaps and grabs. Instead he settled on the contractions and pulses of a cumming cock inside his thin transparent body.

I told him I wasn't going to wait for him to cum.

I don't fuck friends.

When, in fact, I just had.

I wanted to leave the stink from all over him and his dripping human pits. The bruises on his face and the cuts in his ass and the paper cuts on his ugly back. And I was still bombed drunk. But I knew I made a fucking bad mistake.

The rape charges. The aggravated sexual assault next to my felony conviction for child pornography. The way he'd preen and ignore me the next time I saw him at the bar and the public way he'd make this into how boring or dangerous I was. I'm not good at receiving or giving pleasure in this way. It makes no great difference to me what these holes I plug do after I've left. My feelings don't depend on acceptance or vanity. I'm obnoxiously selfish and getting older with every drink and quicker and quicker tryst.

I took the isopropyl he offered.

I took the diseased head he slobbered. And the asshole. And his requests for even more. I respond like a magazine article. Like a dog in heat and, since he didn't want a hug or a kiss or the slightest reciprocation for the, apparently, big favor of getting me to cum somewhere other than my darkened fist, more exactly like a flea'd up old beaten drooling dog in heat.

It's not the giving. Not the sharing. All this I know. It's the agreeing.

F9. *From The Chicago Tribune on September 13, 1999 under the headline;* NEIGHBOR'S TIP LEADS TO GIRL

CHAINED IN BEDROOM *and the sub-headline;* RESCUE ENDS YEARS OF ALLEGED TORTURE:

Norco, Calif. – For years, a little girl lived chained to a bed in a darkened room so filled with trash and feces that her mother tried to blanket the putrid smell with baby powder.

17. Always suck balls and nipples. Rarely ass. I use the finger.

This is all you can do. Next to this seething queer's small messy drunk sodden couch, on a lamp table spattered in greasy lube and cheap recreational drugs, laid the cover of *Time* cut away from the rest of the magazine. "WAR ON GAYS". Over a color photo of the fence that Matthew Shepard got pretty much dead on and imposed over that yet another reproduction of the famous Matt profile inside a thick black obit border.

The needing hole said he was going to hang the cover on his wall somewhere. He said this before he took his clothes off and before I did the same. He said we probably both liked the cover but for different reasons. Probably. Right. As he looked for a newer bottle of headcleaner and a couple of glasses for the supermarket vodka he had sitting on the floor.

Last night he asked me to put cigarettes out on his arms. Like James Dean liked. Like Richey Manic.

James Dean, I think, liked to have cigarettes stubbed out on his chest. But, of course, the other bar faggots in his neighborhood wouldn't be able to see the tattooed scars on his chest while he walked down the shopping street or ordered a cup of hang-over coffee the next day. I suggested I put the hot boxed butts out inside his anus. But I didn't smoke. And the cheezy game words made me cringe. And we were in a restroom in the back of a fag bar with my pants down and his face into my fat gut.

He had asked me to call him JonBenet, if I liked, as we went up the stairs to his apartment on the second night. I told him not to be ridiculous.

He put lipstick on. This time. And insisted. I told him he looked more like Matthew Shepard and that he should start talking even more effeminately.

My time just went cheaper and uglier and more desperate with every word uttered from either mouth.

F10. *From The Chicago Defender, September 11, 1999;* 6-YEAR-OLD GIRL CHAINED TO BED 5 YEARS:

Riverside County sheriff's deputies say the little girl was taken to Loma Linda Medical center after being discovered Tuesday in a harness that was chained to her bed in a room filled with trash and human waste.

And:

They said she had filthy, matted hair down to her waist and could communicate only by moans and whimpers.

And:

The mother told deputies her daughter had been chained to her bed since the age of 1.

18. In rest rooms they show it. In the book stores you ask if it's OK to watch the movie with them. Most are straight and drop their pants to the floor. Most are from the working class.

Advocate: "And do you believe that?"
Judy Shepard: "Well, it's not Matt. It's not the Matt I know, and it's not the Matt other people know."
(Matt's mom being interviewed by Jon Barrett for her cover story in the March 16, 1999 issue of *The Advocate*: A MOTHER'S MISSION.)

F11. *Every single eyebrow hair should be tweezed out one fast clean tug at a time. Her bare brow; her face will slowly start to swell from the pain and abuse and tears and worry. And the little tiny cuts where your clumsy tweezing pulls and pinches and bites her reddened flesh will be what you'll have to cover later. After you've showed her. After you've explained what it means to look down deep inside yourself and find the new hidden sexualities and persona*

you want to explain and explore. The all new yous.

19. I'm in good health, 5'7", 140 lbs. Light brown hair. User friendly.

I like to watch others fuck animals. Degraded women in the sinkhole of their lives who can do nothing but this. That have been reduced to this. Take forty more loads of masturbated cum onto their faces rather than straight down their gullets only because of money marketed laws and civil statutes. Children softened up by selfish ideas too huge and heavy to comprehend just yet. I don't do it. I'm not so fucking depleted that I'll fuck dogs or suck off horses for cash, for lack of looks, for lack of passionate self respect.

And I take this cunt's bottle of headcleaner and stuff it into my fogged head and arteries and shitted asshole and everything his hung mouth could swallow, bite and peck on.

F12. The boy persuaded his sister to enter an abandoned house and "to some degree directed the activities of the others", officials said.

Seven boys – ages 6 to 13 – are suspected in the attack. Police questioned three on Monday at an elementary school and the others Tuesday.

The victim and her attackers were "playmates", police said.

Police said four of the boys, including her brother, raped the girl.

(BOY, 9, LED GANG RAPE OF SISTER, POLICE SAY. *Chicago Tribune, September 22, 1999.*)

20. I always tell them they got a nice Dick. As for sucking, I go all down, off and on, also run the tongue around the head and push it in the hole.

Mothers don't know unless you tell them. Unless someone else, maybe, shoves the information under their noses. They'll stay sad and blind and think that everyone except

the ultimate evil abuser and the tabloids feel the exact same way they do until they see what else is out there. Under the right rocks.

And it is better that they don't know, isn't it? You can get away with all of the dirty terrible thoughts inside your head and underwear this way.

Our child. The words they use slither even better out of your mute straining face.

But mothers and fathers are the only ones that really matter. They change fantasy into flesh, as best as you can get it, they rend sex from ugly self-contained safety. Because what difference does it make: You with your splotched pants down around your ankles, mumbling about what a filthy slut the paid pig on your porno television screen is. Giggling to your fellow internet drips about your autographed copy of ORDEAl: "If she only knew what I was really thinking." Telling me about your girlfriend and the way she swallows.

F13. *Explain that they'll be able to sell this. That they'll be paid to recreate it in tears. This could be left to live on forever under all that new mommy make-up lifestyle.*

Whisper in the pretty little girl's tiny ear by brushing her long mommy decided hairstyle behind her neck. That any earring she wears when she gets old enough to want them will always feel like your hot wet breath. And lick her. To see if she feels it tickle inside her tight bald cunt. Yet.

Tell her: Kneel down. Careful not to smudge your lipstick on your hands. Open your mouth. Lean into your brother. Put your fist full of face, with all your newly discovered accents, into his brand new crotch and open your mouth so that his stubby penis will fit perfectly naturally.

21. I go for build and personality mostly.

Judy Shepard posed for pictures. Looking out into the distance stood fat and puffy in the middle of a huge expanse of sky and sun bleached Wyoming weeds and

flatland; her narrow eyes have a slight gloss. As if she were crying only slightly. Maybe as if the sun were a little too bright.

Another shot like the cover cry that made it across the centerspread of her interview had her looking down at the long weeds and dirty melting snow, her red hair being blown from the cold wind that breezes at her well protected back. In both shots she's got her chubby little hands tucked into her open jacket pockets. On the cover she looks up and out. Inside, she looks down and tired.

Her exclusive poses and interview – five months after her son's murder – is interrupted, first, by a four page advertisement for Fortovase (Saquinavir); an HIV drug marketed by Roche pharmaceuticals, and then by four different full page color ads from four different viatical or viatical-related companies.

Between the HIV drug and the very first viatical ad comes another shot of Judy returning safely to the scene:

Judy at the fence used to corral picketeers during the funeral.

F14. *If she doesn't stop crying soon, use the tweezers to pinch at her little pink nipples hard. Hold them tight and split them open to bleed and scream. And we're not going to stop any of this until he pees. Til he gets hard again. Til he decides he's worried as much for his sister as he is for himself. Use the steely tweezers on his little penis and tight bunched frightened sac. Little cuts and slices and stabs when it becomes uncontrollable. Let that bright raging red burning up their child faces spread down across their flat heaving chests and into their shaking furious nothing little claws.*

22. 3 to 5 minutes and longer.

Throughout the article, there are three small grey photos of our little Matt carefully placed alongside the larger color shots of mother Judy. The last shot of him in a fashion mock sees him staring off into the promising distance, away from the photographer, and now, due to romantic

art direction, the distance has become his parents' beleaguered faces in attentive media close-up:

Dennis and Judy Shepard at a preliminary hearing held last November for Aaron McKinney, one of two men accused of robbing Matthew and beating him to death.

Matthew always looks clumsy and frail and faggy in the few photos his parents have shared with the various medias. Uncomfortable and droopy. There was something slightly jagged about him. In the shots, his mouth seems especially wide and long for such a small shouldered young adult boy. His fair mousey hair always a bit tussled, his eyes dark, his complexion spotty, his cheeks and jowls sunken and thin. He took medication for depression and anxiety and had an eating disorder and told his mother he suffered from nightmare flashbacks caused by a rape that he said occurred in Morocco.

F15. *Twenty years from now and she's old enough to know better but lucky enough to have the queen's excuse and she finds herself flat on her lazy naked back on a mattress on the floor of a Florida hotel room. Ten or so naked dripping males all pushing and shoving for warm wet shots at her paid face and her spread cunt getting plugged one after another. One fat humped faceless nigger slides out greasy and another immediately squats down, slides in far too easy, and pumps in a whole new rhythm without, oddly enough, missing a beat between them. Her cunt is that slack. That weakened. That unkempt. That slippery. That opened and ready. For the next ape to follow the last.*

Another nigger edges his bulky way in between two men who were shovelling their half-hard cocks into her bumbling tongue and soak attempts. He's ready to cum having beat himself off in the back corner better than she could, what with all these hungry lumps crawling all over her, and he wants to deposit it into her mouth. He grabs her head with one huge hand on the back of her sweat soaked hair and yanks her face into his fat belly where his other hand keeps a furious stall on his hard-on. He drops his meaty hard weight painfully into her mouth

and cum jerks all his dysgenic filth into her tight full mouth, straight down into her gagged throat. As he pulls out, stretching and smearing the last drips and spurts onto her recoiled tongue, the director from off-screen shouts for her to clean the shaft.

23. I prefer cut cocks, but they will not turn me off if they are uncut.

I forced my fist into his sparkling red mouth. He was crying then and scared and as hard and tense as he could get. He was sweaty and smeared and flushed.

"Do you see?"

And:

"That's what you taste like."

And:

"Do you do that when I'm not here – do you eat your own shit? You do, don't you? Tell me the truth."

I felt my cock pulsing and stopped my ass from grinding into his little body. His rectum clenched tighter around my cock so he could feel the jerks and spurts and shots of my cum being emptied straight into his stomach. He closed his eyes as if this was a moment of safety and spiritual connection; as if this was what we were both here for.

And he was right; he was perfectly safe. I didn't want to piss in him or all over his nice living room and his drug and shit stank couch. I'm not a teenaged nigger. I pulled out slick and sick and wet brown and green filthy and palmed my hand over my sore balls and cock and wiped down the rest on his pale pink splotched chest. I patted his face. And moved to get dressed as soon as I could rise up off of him.

He laid flat and started to masturbate a little. Ready to cum.

F16. *She didn't end up here. She starts here. She started here. Never pure and innocent. She didn't have the potential. She sees nature from here. This is where the definition rings finally true. This is where it all makes sense.*

24. Reading magazines, TV, music, camping, walks.

There is nothing attractive about Matthew Shepard. Except for his mouth. And the lies that fell out of it on the messy way to find something to fill it. His hungry pretentious past. And his mother.

You look for things. You find them under rocks. Maybe against your will or better judgement.

The crime that took Matthew Shepard's make-believe life was pedestrian. It took him six days in a hospital coma after one full night of blood and pain and hard adult crying strapped to a fence in the plummeting cold weather to die. But there was no sexual assault. And, contrary to the specialized gay communities and lonely fag hag humanists who desperately need such a very safe martyr, not even a hate crime formed from his over-aggressive brand of campy straight cruising.

It is most likely that he was killed in the speed haze of a robbery for fear of identification. It is even more possible that Matthew left the bar where he met the two rough trade white trashes who would pistol whip him into a week long death to cop speed rather than to get double fucked. His new HIV recklessness might have had more to do with extra drugs than extra sex. Which is sexy.

The hits I took from the kid drugs felt weak on top of the drunk that already blurred my vision and affected my balance. The plastic bottle under my nose felt like his shampoo bottle. And the limp effect – smelling what he gave me – was the exact same kind of queen act as his picking a special wash or perfume.

I don't get any more of what little I had earlier this evening or late last night in the bar restroom.

The games he wants to play get played whether I want to or not. His JonBenet lipstick and his gender problems and his Matthew Shepard mouth are all over me wherever I'm at now.

F17. And then she adjusts her bra before she goes. And fixes her make-up for the daylight still outside. After she's

bathed herself of all the extra male filth. All that heavy
white cum and stinking sweat rolls and grabbing and
digging and shoving and sliding all over one after another
as if it mattered what number it was. She checks to see
what her smile looks like in this particular shade that she
thought looked nice for the price in the special make-up
store on the northside. Whatever's most comfortable.

25. It is still thrilling. The cocks are just as good as ever.

Matthew Shepard's mother sets up the bridge between
paedophile and child. Just like all mothers. And regardless
of Matthew's age, the overly darling misfit Matthew that
Judy sells continues to be just a little child. One discovering
and fumbling with his sexuality and forced into creating
fronts that mothers like to say are brave and difficult.
Advocate: "There were some things about gay people that
embarrassed him, though, right?"
Judy Shepard: "Yes. I can only think of one specific
instance. In general, it was the stereotypical gay bars with
sex going on rampantly in the bathrooms. But there was
one specific instance in a park, and it really angered Matt.
He said, 'That's just whoring, and it sets back people's
views on gay relationships so far that it brings forth the
stereotypical view of gay men and that they're incapable of
having a committed relationship – a monogamous,
committed relationship.' He was really upset about it."

F18. I don't hate women and I can fuck children. I can't
imagine any single form being special on its own. I fuck
myself. So few of the things have their own names. So few
are different from the most simple and available form of
nothing pornography.

26. About twice.

Judy Shepard belongs perfectly in the *Advocate*. She
belongs on the cover and in the celebrated middle of such
a thin glossy niche marketed organ for assimilationist

homosexuals. She was made to fit between HIV drug and viatical ads. And she was absolutely correct in her decision to be photographed in a field just like the one her son was found beaten and bleeding and as near to death as it would take six more days and as many doctors and networks to complete.

The context for Matthew Shepard's life and his tiny little death has become the myth of hope that the fractured and desperate gay sympathy dolls just fucking love. That Saint Judy shit. With even more gore. And the dramatic flair that the only two spots on Matthew's face that weren't covered in blood was where his tears had cut long paths sets up so perfectly.

And as many writers as can find room to make the case for Matthew's beatification through his suffering the ultimate homophobic horror, so too are there an equal amount that struggle even harder to lionize the misfit for the unwise, though sadly human, lust that drives so many of their community into quivering hells of hot danger and witty anecdotes.

I got a headache from the creeping sickness and pungent shit mess and deep noisy opened orifices. And the liquor. And before I leave. Before I walk down those fucking stairs back into my answers and bad sleep, I figure I better go into the wretch's bathroom and vomit. So I do. And my lipsticked feces soaked naked friend watches me. And I'm older now and fatter and full of stomach cancer and lymph HIV and can't hold my alcohol as well as I could years and years and just months ago.

"Do you want to sit down awhile?"

The puke that flies from my gut is brown like shit and flecked with red from alcoholism and general bad health and reeks more biting now from this queer's insides than just my own.

But your head clears after you've cleaned out your body from all that slosh. Or, at least, that's what you hope. Now with your adrenalin slipping.

G. WHAT DO YOU THINK IS REPLACED BY PORNOGRAPHY?

G1. *It's never been about masturbation aids, proxy, parallel universes or overly generous credit. Pornography is almost always an old, beaten, loosely rolled funnel. And the long center of which is of little importance. It's what's on the edges that is worthwhile. What goes in and what comes out. The pigs that are formed by it. The pigs that deserved to be changed by letting themselves slide all the way down deep into themselves. Pornography becomes sex because you learn how to safely stick your finger into cinema verité. People become my own personal private smear.*

27. I would not say it is an advantage, but just as good as any other life there is to be had and I've really enjoyed life and will to the end. I'm not lonely, very seldom get bored and I don't buy the sin bit. I'm just as good as anyone, maybe better than a hell of a lot of them.

Judy Shepard, it turns out, didn't know her son even enough to act like she knows him now. And the gay press – especially Jon Barrett, whose cover story interview with Judy follows his previous cover story of Matt as "The Ultimate Ex-Gay" – isn't going to explain it to her.
     Barrett's questions and his frame – "A MOTHER'S MISSION" and Are you surprised to find yourself an activist? – are as safe as a bereaving mother deserves, apparently, regardless of the glaring truths. Judy hasn't even begun to set up the charming Matthew Shepard Foundation for which this interview is the ostensive bow:
Advocate: "Do you have ultimate goals in mind?"
Judy Shepard: "Actually, we're so far in the beginning that I don't even have those yet. I just want to make a positive difference. Even if it only lasts a year, I feel we will have affected more people than already have been – that we will reach people somehow."

G2. *Children that didn't ask for anything better. Because they don't know anything better. Children that never learned.*

28. Yes, off and on and once a group of 10.

All sex is games. Little games that used to cheer on little kids and now take up nearly all the time adults have when they have nothing like god or jobs to keep them busy.

And this skinny hurt queen who wouldn't dare masturbate his naked dog cock in front of me as I hunch over his toilet thinks that the game includes all that phony concern and gossipy care that anyone still lonely for high school days falls for.

"You oughta wipe that lipstick off your face before I do it for you."

G3. *A universal plan with no societal remedy. Please. Squalor that smells perfectly natural. All these snide derisive critiques of suburban living that end right back at the exact same morals and needs; simply reexamined and fashionably tarted down. A massive lack of protection on all open sides. Like AIDS or rape or child abuse by parents thinking they can never squeeze a quick cum out of piddling little selfish urges and clumsy rearing lessons unless there's a unified code of respect and love and altruistic good faith.*

29. Yes. I met them in a bus station rest room and took them to the wood.

What kind of moronic fuck wants a child to look like its mother? Older? You don't put make-up on its pretty little untouched cheeks to hide wrinkles or creases that don't exist. Yet. Until. You pinch its little fatty extras and make them blush pinker; don't you? If you want to see it pinker. The harder you pinch, the redder it gets. Using your frustrated heat like the steel fingers of a wrench, you can make it go from your mom's bundle of trusting wonder to screaming frightened angry demon. Little cunt. Hurt and angry and sad defenceless. Rubbing itself. Little baby cunt.

You dab your finger with its mother's bright red hooker lipstick and simply glide your stained fingertip along the baby's bottom lip. Or you make her kiss as you paint.

You explain to her about how she'll have to learn this later from someone who actually knows what she's doing. You smear the excess between thumb and forefinger and then brush whatever hasn't dissipated across her cheeks in two slow tight drags. This is another way to do it.

There. Now. Sweetheart. Lovely. Perfect.

You're being very good. Aren't you?

What if she does it all by herself? All alone. In her mother's bedroom playing, being bratty and lost in her mess. Of course, it only works, she instincts, if mom and dad see her. If she impresses.

The hand that tenderly placed the kleenex between her newly deepened red lips is the same old man's hand that petted her cheek and stroked her jaw into just as tenderly spreading her tiny mouth open just a bit wider. The mind that patiently waited for her to close her mouth on the tissue to blot the waxy cocksucker advertising she so stupidly crumbled across her stubby teeth and into the insides of her hot tiny mouth with her little pink anxious tongue is the same mind that knew to have the box of selected extra-soft facial tissues purchased and near-by. Even wider. With a wince, finally; that pre-pubescent act of strain that tells me and her invisible constant audience the incredibly tiresome extent of her tiny princess favor. Of how nice she was being. Of how she deserved more than just flattery. How her halo-d praise was earned. Now. See. How the acknowledgements and pets and pats are fully owned now.

Sweetheart. Honey.

Perfect.

You're being just the most beautiful doll; aren't you? Aren't you?

It's better this way. This is the best way.

How does this look on an old hag like me?

Light blue wisps of comforting tissues. Like putting your hand between fat warm furs, I'd imagine. Being hugged and safe pre-fucked maybe. The size of an adult's used snot wad stuck with the hideous imprint of its aged pinched and falled dragged open lipsticked black pit.

Does this make me in any way even the slightest

hope more acceptable?

The brushed gentle red testament to a child's natural greed. A miniature version of the old rag whore deep inside. All waiting to be paid. Or worse.

The size of the child's smack could be swallowed by the fisted blot of the adult's. So, to use it later, he folds the tissue, ruining it of course, and stuffs it in his front pants pocket. Near his dick. Let me show you something else.

You make it look like a cunt.

G4. *A documentary on a porn star that killed herself seems to shy away from the blunt stupidity of the typically cute girl who used what little she had lifted from the usual morass of neglect and haywire vanity. And in the last days of her blonde hollywood life, Savanah comes to perform a gang bang with eight men. This is presented as her nadir:*

"For someone who had become a near legend in the adult film industry, StarBangers was a desperate act by a desperate woman."

And

"StarBangers #1 briefly revived Savanah's fame but Savanah was damaged goods. Her phone stopped ringing. And the hottest number in porn was suddenly a has-been at age twenty-two."

30. They just show their Dicks and I ask, you want a BJ, and let's go to a safe place.

You work it all out again and again. Just like the acts themselves.

This last trip to London included a stop to one of these Soho beasts that advertise by putting up a piece of paper on the outside stairwell of their rent-a-room walk ups:

New. Friendly. Busty.

The details get flattened into one another.

I masturbated in front of her. As she laid on the bed I refused to even sit on. I stood at the foot of the low bare mattress and watched her dig her fingers inside her

over-grown adult cunt. Her idea. And I jerked off because it was the way for both of us to know when I should leave. Quickly.

I cummed on the carpet and in my fist. She made some garbled English comment about how she likes to see a clean cock do what its supposed to do; just not on her floor.

She suggested I clean myself up before I leave. Though I'm hardly a stranger to just dropping my load in my hands and underwear and all over my coat, I waited for her to finish first. As I hadn't touched her, this was probably just her ritual. She walked by me, friendly like they all are, naked, and started to ask questions about where I was from and what I was doing there. She apologized about the weather and I explained to her where Chicago was.

Naked she was revolting.

Naked and yapping.

Naked and sunk and drooping and sucking her only slight paunch in even though we were done and washing her cunted hands in the small sink as I stood outside her opened door toilet in the room designed just for this.

You remember it differently each time.

You don't put make-up on a child to make her look older. You put it on to show her off. Look at this fucking thing.

You teach it to look in the mirror and check. Then turn to the queue. Smile. Take it all in.

These mules behind all these stairs and doors and tips are called models, if not euphemistically by themselves, then at least, by the marketed punters.

Make-up is for the audience. It's what you use to smirk at others who you think need to know about your interests. What you're going to do to the one you're painting.

Happy Birthday, Darling.

You don't dress up a little vulnerable to look less vulnerable do you? To look more than less pre-teen. Closer to hag. Closer to mom. Closer to the anachronism of what

you're doing with what.

Did you miss your chance? Are you like every other cocksucker out there who just wants a hug and a womb and confuses the absolutely absent relationship between the two.

You don't live your life this way, do you?

You step off the street, follow the dark stairs to the top, guessing which door is simply safest, quickest, best. And they are, no matter how entertaining the memory afterwards, exactly all the same. Whether you fuck it or not. Or whatever you call it – whatever it is that you do there.

And all the kids run by your embarrassed face, as your eyes are fixated down on your sloppy cock and grinding fingers.

All their ages and the crimes against them and precisely where the combination seems utterly perfect.

It gets easier. And it gets older.

This is exactly how child molesters get off. In their hands. There are no screams, no scissors and tape, no cameras and no long lists of new problems. I didn't do it and there's nothing better.

It's Fisher Price commercials. Gap Kids.

It's "Be gentle with me" and the overly sensitive acquiescence. It's exculpatory evidence before the fact.

Little cunt. Our child.

The words are just simple noises. Too fucking easy. They form in my head and blur out of my mouth far too quickly. Little retarded cunt. Little cunt. How small is 11 years old, how retarded is that un-grown? Had she lived, would she still be so fuckable? Retarded like that. Cute at that unsafe age.

G5. *You don't masturbate to hate. You use someone else's hatred. Or obsessions. Or confusion. Never your own. You respond. Not act. You may agree or inculcate. But you never choose or decide.*

31. Most stood and a couple laid down. I was on my knees.

What was JonBenet like without all that lovely make-up?
As a little girl who hadn't had her head bashed in and her
skinny throat squeezed and her bothersome cute little six-
year-old fanny wiping problems. You know that, right?
That she hated wiping herself, right?

G6. *The director of StarBangers, John T. Bone, spoke
briefly in the same documentary (E Hollywood True Stories:
Savanah):*
*"I came up with the idea of taking the world
famous ice queen and putting her into the most intense
pornographic situation that any star would go into. That
was so removed from anything she'd ever done or what
anybody'd conceive she would ever do that it would stand
the industry on its ear.*
I got lucky."

32. No.

I wiped my chin and down my t-shirt with a great wad of
toilet paper and then flushed the toilet for the third
fucking time. I hand wiped the sweat back into my hair
and bent my back as far as I could to try and work the crik
out of my spine. I stopped by his mirror to see how pale
and red eyed I looked and then decided not to.
        He had put on a long black t-shirt and some
flannel shorts and cleaned his face on, I'm guessing, a dish
towel.
        "Sorry. I'm really fucking old."
        He assured me I wasn't, though I'm close to twice
his age. He asked me to sit down and have some coffee.
But I declined. Now politely.
        "You're not worried about re-infection?"
        "No. Frankly. No"
        "How're you doing?"
        "Fine."

G7. *John T. Bone's StarBangers series came somewhere
among his well documented "World's Greatest Gang
Bang" series – where one woman gets penetrated by ever*

greater numbers (251, 300, 500 plus) in as quick a manner as possible – and his various transsexual films. These are the films that I know him from. The films that I've looked for. That have tangentially crossed my well worn path.

33. Most just took their pants down. Two took all their clothes off.

From *The Chicago Tribune*, Saturday, October 10, 1998, under the headline HATE CRIME ALLEGED IN WYOMING ATTACK and the subheadline GAY MAN BEATEN, ROBBED, BURNED:

> Shepard was found Wednesday evening by a man on a bicycle who at first thought he was a scarecrow or a dummy because of how he was tied to the fence.
>
> He was unconscious, and his skull had been smashed with a handgun. He also appeared to have suffered burns on his body and cuts on his head and face. The temperature had dropped into the low 30s during the more than 12 hours Shepard was left outside.
>
> He was on a respirator Friday in a Ft. Collins, Colo., hospital.
>
> "He's a small person with a big heart, mind and soul that someone tried to beat out of him," said his uncle, R.W. Eaton. "Right now, he's in God's hands."

G8. *John T. Bone interviews a young Thai transsexual prostitute, documentary style, at the beginning of his first "Lady Boys" film:*

> *"What is a lady boy?"*
>
> *"What is lady boy? Lady boy, I think, inside, yeah, want to be lady."*
>
> *Lady Boys and Lady Boys #2 begin a theme that would continue in Bone's "Guess What?" and "Guess Again" films. That is: men with slight bodies and effeminate faces in make-up loaded on hormones and gender confusion have sex with men and women who may be fooled – or need to pretend they're fooled – by their actual gender.*

34. All worth blowing. Glad I didn't tire out too fast.

DEATH IN THE WEST – GAY YOUTH ACTIVIST MATTHEW SHEPARD DIED MONDAY AFTER BEING SAVAGELY BEATEN IN WYOMING:
Chicagoans will offer their support to slain gay youth leader Matthew Shepard in a vigil Wed., Oct. 14, 7pm at Waveland and Halsted (wear yellow armbands with green circles).
(*Outlines* [The Weekly Voice of the Gay, Lesbian, Bisexual and Trans Community] Oct. 14, 1998).

BATTERED GAY U. OF WYOMING STUDENT DIES:
Early this morning hospital spokesman Rulon Stacey gave a statement for Shepard's family saying, "He came into the world premature, and he left the world premature."
He added, "Matthew's mother said to me, please tell everybody who's listening to go home and give your kids a hug, and don't let a day go by without telling them that you love them."
(*Chicago Defender*, Oct. 14, 1998).

FRIENDS AND STRANGERS MOURN GAY STUDENT IN WYOMING:
"There is an image that comes to mind when I reflect on Matt on that wooden cross rail fence", the Rev. Royce W. Brown, the pastor of St. Mark's, said in a eulogy. "I replace that image with that of another man hung upon a cross. When I concentrate on that man, I can release the bitterness inside."
Mr. Shepard, a 21-year-old freshman at the University of Wyoming, had dreamed of working one day for human rights. In death, he has become a national catalyst for a new drive to guarantee for homosexuals the right to physical safety.
(*The New York Times*, Oct. 17, 1998).

RALLY FOR SLAIN GAY STUDENT ENDS IN ARRESTS:
Dozens were arrested Monday night in New York

at a protest against hate crimes and the fatal beating of a gay college student in Wyoming. Several thousand people marched in Manhattan, and at least 90 were arrested, most for disorderly conduct, Mayor Rudolph Giuliani said. He said the rally started as a vigil of about 200 people, but the crowd rapidly grew.
(*Chicago Sun-Times*, Oct. 20, 1998).

MAN PLEADS GUILTY IN SLAYING OF GAY STUDENT: Judy Shepard cried at the courtroom podium while talking about her son, then turned to Henderson, "I hope you never experience another day or night without experiencing the terror, humiliation, the hopelessness and helplessness that my son felt that night".
(*Chicago Tribune*, April 6, 1999).

G9. *Bone's Guess films are built around peroxide transsexual Kelly Michaels. Michaels wears its hair short and feathered, wears its tits small, pointy and hormonal, and seems to have a special predilection for loud, thick, matte red lipstick. He also displays a charming tendency towards impotence when he has to fuck women and in both films resorts to faked cum shots when orgasms are required of him. He sloppily squirts something looking like cum out of his fist as he pretends to finish his job manually onto Annabel Chong's face in Guess Again.*

35. It took me about 8 hours for all 15, to have the sex and go back to the rest room and get another.

I had three fingers inside him while I tried hard to discern the senses between mouth and tongue and fist. And he moaned when I tried to fit in a fourth. He clenched his ass and bounced his dripping glistening cock and balls at me. And when I slapped his ass he understood to switch.

And it was wide open and I put my finger straight in, all the way in.

He wanted me to see his lipstick on my hard-on. He wanted to show me his slob work. I had to look down and see his queening and hogging. His drill and his lessons

and his bottom rung pride.

I remembered all this as I tried to faze back into a steady foothold.

All the infection that slid into his tiny wounds and through his slow bloodstream oiling down that opened wide stuffed and aching and straining stinking asshole.

The yeasty thrush like old milk in his mouth stuck into my pisshole and smeared in red turning pink on vodka and beer sweat and fat heaves. His ugly attempts at rhythmic time and mutual satisfaction. Which I am utterly incapable of. If for no other reason than complete unpracticed ineptitude. All the illness. The declining possibilities. There was nothing dangerous. Only sensationalist. And either way it all pissed me off.

He asked me again for a book I had said I would give him later. Yes, I said, next time I see you.

"Have you ever really hurt a child?"

Women think they deserve honesty after they've had sex with someone. Don't act like a woman.

"If I say yes, are you going to get all hard or faggy about it?"

"You're the only one that came."

"Do you have any KP around here?"

"No."

"Have you ever seen it?"

"Yes."

"But you didn't keep it?"

"It's not really so much my thing."

"I can't see how you'd expect me to answer that – at least, where you'd think that I was being totally honest."

G10. *Both Guess films feature pale skinny Michaels having sex with multiple male partners in single encounters. Guess What sees three fat cock'd homosexuals vying for his made-up face and crowding in to stuff only two cocks simultaneously into his small lipstick'd gobbling sucking slobbing mouth. Guess Again trims the crew by one but has Michaels slobbing on the double combination just the same, this time in full drag. At the climax of both scenes,*

Michaels either has his lipstick smeared all over his face or has it completely wiped off by his faggot mouth performance.

36. Both.

Matthew Shepard was a pincushion. And rather a different sort of pincushion than the type his mother needs him to have been.

Matthew Shepard was raped just a little too much during his twenty-one years on this planet. His prescriptions might prove that his mother wanted to believe the details – she only really concerned herself with the first one in Morocco – but in light of all the new coming information being fed slowly and begrudgingly through the cracks in the people who would seem to protect her, how much longer before she changes her mind on the life that her son really did live. And, of course, that'll only hurt her more. Like a mother. Who tried. She'll understand that it must have been even more difficult for tiny him to have thought he must make up lies and moral fibs and brave fronts all these short truly wasted years before her. Because her love and compassion and sympathy and worry for his – very tenuous – safety were unconditional. Though, apparently, he didn't know that. And she couldn't see through it.

G11. *Michaels, with his short hair and his struggles to stay hard, can be supplanted by Matthew Shepard. With the two cocks being shoved into his mouth. With the lipstick, mother, and the low requirement that he had to end up there sooner or later.*

37. My neck and jaw only.

Judy Shepard could see what her boy was before he was found dead. I see it every week almost.

Judy Shepard tells the communities looking for themselves in her son that there's a warm place for all of them. And I know she's perfectly correct. All the desperate

noise reassures me. As does seeing all these horny martyrs crawling in the cummed-up dirt that they shovel over themselves again and again.

G12. *Matthew Shepard was not killed because he was gay. His slippery mouth was made for tattling as much as it was for fellating. But his murder's incredible resonance has the same appeal, albeit in lesser quantities, of transsexual pornography. That is; Exploited gender confusion under thick globs of misfiring howling peacocked frailty. Sold damage. Sold fucked finality.*

38. Just friendly teenagers. Some said thanks, some said they enjoyed it, some said I could suck it all day.

MATT'S HIV STATUS:
        In a long article about Shepard, writer Melanie Thernstrom reported that the AIDS virus was found in Shepard's blood when he was being treated after the attack. "The infection, detected in the hospital, was thought to have been a very recent one", Thernstrom writes. She says that Shepard had not told his friends or his mother he was positive and likely did not know himself. (*The Advocate*, John Gallagher, March 16, 1999).

G13. *It is most probable that John T. Bone sought to fit his transsexual and gang bang videos into a specific market. The bisexual or, more accurately and pathetically, the bi-curious market would do well with both series. Quiet self-hating queers, frat boys and misogynists. Bored heterosexuals and bored faggots all just slightly angry over their circumscribed lack of potential.*

39. The rain started on the last one, but I kept sucking till he shot and we were both drenched, but he didn't seem to mind and said it was great.

SHEPARD CLAIMED RAPE:
        Slain gay student Matthew Shepard reportedly claimed two months ago that he was raped by three men

during an alcohol-blurred outing near Yellowstone National Park.

But Park County, Wyoming, sheriff's deputy Scott Steward tells *The Denver Post* today that tests showed no signs of sexual assault and Shepard decided not to press charges.
(*Chicago Defender*, Oct. 17, 1998).

G14. *In a typically safe fanboy interview, "adult film" director Patrick Collins talks about John T. Bone:*
"He's the kind of guy that'll go to a girl and say, 'You know what, you don't wanna do anal, but I really need an anal scene'. Or he'll hire her and know he's going to do an anal scene with her, and he'll just offer her a little more money or whatever he has to do to get her to do it, and she'll end up feelin' like a whore afterwards. So he's one of the low-life punks in this business that, when *Inside Edition* or *48 Hours* or *20/20* or any of these shows do a story, you know they always want to focus on the assholes like Bone and some of these other pricks that are misogynous and have absolutely ...(getting upset) they couldn't give a shit about any of the people in this business. They only care about themselves."
(The X Factory, Anthony Petkovich, Critical Vision, 1997)

40. Most I went through with it, as the meat was too nice to let go. Some bothered me and some I told I had a sore tooth so I just jerked them off. Once I ended up with four Army men when my buddy left as he was afraid. Once a guy left me miles from the city and it was cold, 15 degrees, but I got a ride. Once two young moving van drivers took me in the van on the mats for sex. While I sucked one I played with the other, and then sucked both dicks at one time.

The March 1999 issue of *Out* had two articles on Matthew; the second of which was "Writing The Book Of Matthew" by Elise Harris where the heated prurient could learn that Matthew "had several black lovers" and "went to parties and a public park where local gay men and

lesbians hung out" and that "he dated a lot; during his time in Denver, he saw a 35-year-old African-American pharmacist, a 35-year-old deaf-mute, and a 23-year-old crystal meth dealer."

I turn all these cheap repeated ideas into pornography. I smell the boy being used and using his youth and getting AIDS for drugs. Bottom feeders. Easy fucks and simple settled payments. I check the mother pretending to have been concerned only now. I can guess why she wants to. They're just words and words are the easiest thing to let drip out of your mouth when no one is going to hold you accountable.

I turn all these rutting acts into pornography. I see these carnalities and memories in the same flat manner as I see all these ridiculous characters and their lying hyena lives. They're only as good as I decide well before hand. The pleasure is in looking as hard as you can until the pictures break down into mere dots and motives.

In "A Boy's Life" by JoAnn Wypijewski from the September 1999 issue of *Harper's*, I learn that my vague over-excited picture of the suffering bleeding pistol whipped young gay man wasn't as precise as I trusted:

His hands were not outstretched, as has been suggested by all manner of media since October 7, 1998, when the twenty-one-year-old University of Wyoming student was discovered near death, but rather tied behind him as if in handcuffs, lashed to a pole four inches off the ground. His head propped on the lowest fence rail, his legs extending out to the east, he was lying almost flat on his back when Deputy Reggie Fluty of the Albany County Sheriff's Department found him at 6:22 pm, eighteen hours, it is believed, after he was assaulted.

I don't want his coffee or his time. And I'm not especially sorry that the words he chooses to play with are the same ones I've heard over and over this long many years. I think to ask him about his mother and turn her into Judy to his Matthew but I think better against it.

"Do you still want to cum?"

"I'm OK."

"You sure?"

"Why – what do you want?"

I'm reeking of vomit and shit and old alcohol stained flesh. I'm fat and grey and drunk and sloppy and so pathetic that I can get hard again as soon as I think my head's the slightest bit cleared of embarrassment and self-respect. Or shame.

"I want to wrap that photo of Matthew Shepard around your cock and cut both of you into little bits."

"I really want to keep that photo."

I have every intention of wiping his fuck thicked asshole with it. Of wadding it up into a pointy little ball and shoving it up the slickened rut I fit three painful dripping fingers into.

Once two young moving van drivers took me in the van on the mats for sex. While I sucked one I played with the other, and then sucked both dicks at one time.

"You understand the real difference between what you're doing – how rude and measly you're being – and what JonBenet was? Or were you just being a faggot? Just being campy and trying to be outrageous? I hate faggot comedians."

And:

"The difference is she was six."

And:

"How come you don't have a photo of her around here?"

That's what you do with pornography. You return to it. You keep it. If it means something more to you than just a single simple cum. Which is what sex is. Too much work and too much empty kid stuff. You don't do a fucking thing – you don't do anything after a certain age. Except keep looking. At less than nothing. At less and less. Nothing new. And everything is potential pornography. So you're always just busy.

"I wish you had a picture of JonBenet around here. This place could use a little brightening up. You like little six-year-old girls, don't you?"

And:

While I sucked one I played with the other, and then sucked both dicks at one time.

200

And:

Put it in. If you don't keep that hand down, I'll slit your neck. Put it in.

And:

Just put it in now, love. Put it in now.

And:

Put it in your mouth and keep it in and you'll be all right.

And:

Can I just tell you summat? I must tell you summat. Please take your hands off me a minute, please. Please – mummy – please.

I can't tell you.

I can't tell you. I can't breathe. Oh.

I can't – dad – will you take your hands off me?

And:

Please God.

And:

Tell me.

And

I can't while you've got your hands on me.

And:

Monday, October 30, 1989.

Didn't sleep at all. Sucked him five or six times, masturbated ten or fifteen times, crotch fucked six or seven times. 2:00 a.m. He woke up – didn't seem to mind being nude. I pulled him up on top of me – his belly to mine, my cock in his crotch. He slept on top of me for half hour as I rubbed his back and butt. Was able to give him good erection as he slept.

2:45 a.m. He woke up. I made him suck me about five seconds before going back to sleep.

3:15 a.m. Said, "I'm going to kill you in the morning." He said, "No, you're not." I said I wouldn't before he started crying too loud.

And:

Her head wasn't touching the floor. Her skirt fell down and I could see the hole in her vagina was gaping, like it must have been well relaxed, and it was wide open and I put my finger straight in, all the way in. I took it out

again, just the once, and I laid her down on the floor and masturbated. When I'd done that I put her knickers back on.

G16. *Annabel Chong's real name is Grace Quek. She features in many of Bone's films including the first World's Greatest Gang Bang and both Kelly Michaels vehicles. She tells an interviewer in the Oct/Nov 1999 issue of Show that, while studying art in London, she was gang raped. She says her attackers received only a few months of jail for the attack but that she won a settlement in a civil suit.*
    In another brief, largely empty, interview in Pop Smear magazine from Sept/Oct 1999, Annabel was asked if she got chafed during the (video'd) gang bang:
    "It was ...yeah, at some point I started to feel the strain of it, but in the video you see John Bowen (T. Bone) announcing to the guys that I was scratched up. It was not true: They just wanted the guys to go easy on me. It was a little insane."
    In a David Aaron Clark film, Asianatrix, made after Annabel left John T. Bone's company, the slight asian continues her stellar reputation in a bukkake segment.

41. I was in a park. It was entrapment. He was a college kid. He asked me for a light, I gave him one, but he came extra close to me. I walked away and he came up again. I felt his meat. It was hard. He then pulled out his badge and said I was under arrest. All he said after that was, don't you read the papers. 14 were trapped that week. I said I was out of town. I figured I was ruined so I said to myself I'll fight it all the way, as the other 14 got 6 months and/or $200 fine and their names in the paper. I got out on bail after 3 hrs. and had an Atty. in another city, who knows I'm gay. In court I told the judge it was an accident; I stated my back was to him and he came up so close it startled me and when I turned around my hand brushed him. The vice cop was not at court. I pleaded to suspicious person and was fined $20. The Atty. was $200. It didn't hurt me otherwise.

The 9-year-old known as Girl X confirmed her attacker's identity with a nod of her head about six months after she was raped and nearly strangled in her Cabrini Green apartment building, her mother said during a pre-trial hearing Monday. Patrick Sykes was charged in April 1997 with predatory sexual assault in the Jan. 9, 1997, attack on the fourth-grader. She can't speak, is partially blind and uses a wheelchair because of her injuries. Prosecutors are asking a judge to allow the mother's testimony under a law that lets parents and teachers speak on behalf of sexual assault victims under age 13. (HEARING IN GIRL X CASE, Chicago Sun-Times, September 28, 1999).

G17. *How rare it is that a victim gets to recreate its life as short commodified scenes. Matthew Shepard's mother trying hard to grasp what truth she can handle by getting further and further from any actual sense of her son's flimsy reality. Grace cloaking herself in more and more direction and mouthing soft and immediate lies in interviews as herself squatting on her character. John T. Bone's filmed fantasies bearing more flesh than, say, his paintings would do. Artists constructing ideals out of desperation by twisting their limited experience into crude guileful quilts. Limply arguing possibilities when they mean daydreams. Masturbating. Loudly. And still peeking.*

G18. *I have pictures of crouched women in peep show booths. Things from some internet site somewhere; some magazine, some fucking video club. The women are using glory holes cut between the walls. Long thick porno size cocks are shoved through for the models to lick, swallow or feel. Tooling the men off or getting ready to put their mouths on whatever is exposed.*
    The women are naked in every single shot. Their tits in better view when they're just fist jerking the disembodied cocks rather than shoving their heads all over them.

G19. *There is no equanimity. I see no unity. Not among*

low-lifes. I don't judge the bird's nests and short shaved heads by the inflated obsessives in movies and porn screens. Though I suspect they do. These degenerates have tattoos and decide hairstyles. Many of them actually have given up. But I know they care. Still. They've been beaten down to this. They've learned to pretend hard. They play at self-control and pretend to lose. They sleep and peck at convenient addictions. Motherly excuses. Corporeally.

And yet they all think they fool you by acting as if they don't mind. That sex is no big deal. Sex is simple shared fun. Sex is instinctive and essential. While the hanging grade they fail to make oozes from every small sense of belonging they ever hoped to claw, drag, hide or ignore.

G20. Three Advocate covers for Matthew Shepard in the first year of his death; the last one celebrating the first anniversary of his murder. The last two with exclusive interviews with Matthew's mother. These have a function. Such a common crime on such a common little beggar. All blown up to include all those who'll also never matter.

G21. It's important to know that the women in these male places are, in fact, women. Their loathsome breasts and long primped hair and fat cunts twisting the ashtray eroticism of such places into a hate crime.

The pornographic context is changed. Not just by simple gender. Or by societal roles or inequities. By requirement. Act. Delivery. But also by audience. By their blunt obvious choices.

G22. The child sits on the bed that smells like the cheap sex her parents perform in her memory. Lay back. Lay all the way back. Spread your legs wide. As wide as this. Take the tweezers and pull at her tiny labia. That hasn't given away to thick folds of used meat and wear. Find her baby clit. And squeeze. Between the teeth. Her nubbed flesh inside closed tight cosmetic metal on metal. Pull up whatever hasn't burst into blood and detached skin. Sink the steel tips in again. Grind down. Fuck it. Push it straight

down through the uppermost tip of her dirty disgusting female speciality. Say: You don't need it. You don't need any of it. Any of this.

Let her live that way. Reduced. People become pornography. Choices become demands. Demands become personalities. Let her live like Mary Vincent.

G23. There are nineteen photos detailing the reverend Jimmy Swaggart's specific tastes around a New Orleans prostitute in the July 1988 issue of Penthouse.

The photos are in grainy black and white when they should be in full color. But the photographer may have been trying to make the shots of the bedraggled whore and her low ball surroundings look as seedy as they felt. Or pretend that it's news. Or perhaps; he was trying to separate these shots, as much as possible, from the airbrushed soft-focus diego style of the other women that fill the pages of Penthouse. But more probably he was struggling to clean up the hairy sloppy wasted beast by flattening her out just a little. While still conveying what a pig it was that the anti-porn crusader would settle – or look – for.

There are close-ups of her chewed up cunt. Her thick black pubic nest spiralling out and down into greasy clumps in her ass and across her flabby fat flat buttocks. Her inner thighs and hips and upper arms are seen to be streaked in mutant gorilla hair. There are close-ups of her poked jail or gang or trash tattoos and her saggy sunken tits. Her stupid smile and paid smirk. Her backwoods dull eyes and flat niggerish barely white nose.

She models her thick waist and her used breasts and her hirsute cunt in the passenger side of a moving car in mimicry of what Jimmy Swaggart used to ask her for. She tugs her fat meaty labia up into her black rat's nest with her short stubby fingernails and then later rends a pair of old white panties up through her split old female cracks. Wearing just the panties, she dogs on all fours atop a motel bed before she squats in front of the empty chair that the reverend used to sit in as he masturbated. She rubs a dildo on the fleshy meat hanging off her gaping pit

underneath all that spidery pubic hair in two separate and unfortunate gynaecologically obsessed close-ups.

G24. *Penthouse called Debra Murphee, when advertising the photo spread and accompanying interview, a* $20 New Orleans prostitute. *In Let Us Prey, a book about Jimmy Swaggart and his tiny problems, she is sold as* the picture of the stereotypical veteran New Orleans prostitute *who almost never smiled and when she did, she kept her lips closed, hiding her uneven teeth. In sum, she was a decidedly unattractive individual, described by many as being ugly or gross.*

G25. *Next to the obligatory photo of the front desk and the sloppy POSITIVELY NO REFUNDS AFTER 15 MINUTES placard at the motel that Debra used as her brothel is the caption:*
"Most people paid me $30 or $40 for a quick blowjob. When I first met him, he offered me $10 to jack off, and I said, 'No', and he said, 'I'm going to do it myself. You won't have to touch me.' And I said, 'No, I won't do anything under $20. Even if you want to look at my titties, you have to give me $20.'"

G26. *Street whores lie to themselves about how much they're getting paid. They can't admit to the nagging dread of losing any one single ugly chance. The possibility that they might not get at least something. No matter how small. No matter how degrading the fact that they would take absolutely anything. And then spend it almost immediately on help. To scrape the value down even more. And to reduce the sting of perpetual valuelessness.*
I told her to just sit there. She watched my hand move around my cock and tended to avoid my eye contact. Probably because she could leave as soon as I came and she knew that a facial expression other than professional hate focus and beaten genetic stupidity might slow me down.

G27. "Or he might have brought the rubbers and let me

keep them. He always brought Trojans Lubricated in the blue pack.... Most of the time when he'd buy them and let me keep them, he'd buy a box of three."

I usually give my unused tokens to the faggots that are still staying behind. I even give them the extra quarters that I've changed at the front counter. The change goes from booth coin box to the till and back again. I drop the condom packs on the floor of the booth or in a garbage bin on the way out towards the door. Sometimes I keep the torn three packs wadded up in my fist throughout the entire dalliance just in case I'll need another.

G28. "He asked me to unbutton my blouse and unzip my pants in the car while he drove around and jacked off."

I know she put herself here. But I accept the excuses as possibilities. And I know I understand very little of the whole story. I get so little this way. Which is fine. Which is perfect. Which explains it all, actually.

G29. *From Transformation – "The Magazine Created For Men Who Enjoy Being Women"; from their interview with their "Boy-Girl Of The Month":*
Transformation: "What do you like most about life as a female?"
Gia Darling: "Being able to turn heads and make men drool when I walk into a room. Believe me, it has happened."
(Transformation #21)

G30. "He'd always try and talk me into pulling my pants off and facing him sideways with my legs spread. I said, 'No, I'm not going to take my pants off in the car. If we get stopped, I won't have time to put them back on.'"

Some were overly friendly or insistent. I don't need any help. Don't stick your fingers inside of you. Stick your tongue out. She knew to jut it in and out of her mouth like she was licking any one of the cocks she never ever worked that way. She'd wiggle it around and dart it at me like a greasy cracked nigger snake.

Don't touch your tits.

You're the only one that needs to be worried about getting caught or mugged. Once inside the front seat, she'd be all quick business. Of course, she's done this a lot more than you and it's also a lot harder for her to wait.

G31. "I'd start standing up, pull my underwear up between my crack, and then he'd tell me to get on my hands and knees and then turn over and take my panties off and play with myself. He said I had a fat pussy and he liked fat pussies."

The words that slur out of these cunts' mouths that are supposed to tell you what you like. As if there is some common bond. As if she knows something naturally true about men. As if she has something extra to offer.

G32. Transformation: "What is the most exciting aspect of being a female to you?"
Olivia Love: "My Beauty."
(Transformation #22)
Transformation: "What is the most exciting aspect of being a female to you?"
Lexus: "Being a female allows me to feel free, and being who I was supposed to be."
(Transformation #23)
Transformation: "What is the most exciting aspect of being a female to you?"
Tara: "Wearing tight clothes, having big boobs and the cat calls from men."
(Transformation #24)

G33. "He just laid on the bed and he said, 'Just stand over me', you know, 'I just wanna peek'. He wanted me to have a dress on, and I'd pretend that he's not there, and then he'd come sneak up and peek up my dress. He just more or less liked to see the lips sticking out my panties and liked it real tight."

G34. *A color photo of Julia Hember titled "Self-portrait*

With Diamond Earrings" is included in the 1998 edition of
the John Kobal Photographic Award catalog. Julia has
numerous slashes and scratches covering her face; across
her nose, across her cheek and up her forehead into her
hairline. Her temple is stained with a thick splotch of blood
and her brown hair is matted and slick with it. There is no
other information in the catalog about Julia's aesthetics or
student opinions and it is most possible that the damage is
very well done make-up. Her eyes are bruised purple.
Another bruise stretches around her slender white neck.
So, of course, Julia is pitching for something closer to
domestic violence or rape rather than a car-crash or a
rough stumble down a fucking long flight of stairs. But
anything is possible. And I like how especially careful it is
no matter what her pretensions.
G35. "I'd ask him if he wanted me to take my clothes off.
He says, 'Yeah, down to your panties'. I'd say, 'How do
you want me?' He'd say, 'Get on your hands and knees on
the bed.' So I would."

G36. This is an ad: Send me your videos. I know you wife
batterers must do it. Send them to me. This is what I want:
both of you. The one beaten up just like a cunt and the
one who did it just like a vain palsy. Talk to each other
from either side of the camera. How it felt and why you're
willing to try again.

Or, ladies, if you've already filed a restraining
order, then tell a girlfriend to help you. You can tell her
everything. How it started and what you were hoping to
accomplish and what, exactly, in detail, failed. And how
you've changed. And show me the scars. And the tears.
The romantic ones and the existential ones. The tears that
start when you talk about remembering the little girl you
were and the messy ones that split through the anger
when you point out the physical pain.

Gentlemen, do this for me: Make a video of you
cutting up the girl that is stupid enough to put on that
make-up for you and stay with you. Tell her. Ask her. Have
your new girlfriend talk about the old wife and what lies
she knows about the reasons you two were ever together.

While this one talks, move in for close-ups of what you like best. As if you were with a market cheap appalachian blonde in the front seat of your car and she asked you if you'd like to see her tits first. And don't forget to itemize your own personal attractions and world weary mistakes. Generalize. Explain. Bark. Convince others as you stumble to convince yourself.

G37. "I was on my knees, doggie-style, with my feet hanging off the bed... He pulled his jogging suit down around his ankles and left his T-shirt on... He stuck it in and pumped a couple of times and pulled it out... He was very easy. A few pumps and that was it. He'd just moan, and as soon as he got done, he'd throw the rubber in the trash, tuck it in, and walk out the door."

G38. *This would be nearer the truth. These men masturbate to the same ideas that their rental audience does. Touching the girl knelt back below them is prohibited by market rules. They can only jerk off over her. The sex act stays at their own speed and motivation as long as they can fit their orgasm into the timeline of the director and his shooting schedule. The girl's knees may hurt. A visible mean of respect must be enforced. You don't let a group of naked men loose on a single female without rules. And all the other men watching and waiting and timing won't help make room or control themselves or mind their turn unless a certain decorum is established. Editing can clean up the pacing but only within a narrow linear/narrative frame. She can't be allowed to sit in the cum too long lest the waste soaks in or otherwise dissipates.*

They look down. At her cleanliness. At her as yet untouched showered willingness. At her low life plans. Then they continue to look down. At her use. As the numbers spend and grow. At the way others have treated her before them. At the way they all treat her and the way she takes it. The way she acts now and how she agreed long ago. The way she needs this for whatever she says and then the real reasons. The way she can't back it up. At

how revolting she is. At the way he can use her. All the
greyhound bums and niggers and donut eaters. Her
middle-level looks if you're feeling kind or generous. Like a
bucket on the outside. And filthier on the inside.

That's what makes you cum. What the producers
and paycheck accountants are banking on. That you'll see
her for exactly what she is. And their professional lighting
and catering skills and financial planning and personal
scheduling all assure that their precious time hasn't been
wasted. When the audience thinks it's worth $3.00 or so a
night until a month later when the next volume and a
different girl might be worth a similar pocket change crack.

G39. "I asked him, 'Do you want a date?' And he said, 'All
I want to do is jack off awhile... look at your tits.'"
You hold her head tight between your hands and
thrust deepest into the hole that keeps your cock in
artificial wet friction while it starts to choke on your
cumming insistence. You don't let it breathe until you're
done. At that moment; you don't care until you're done.
And all your disease and filth is deposited cleanly into
whatever spirituality it uses to pretend what you're doing is
consensual and human.

G40. Yes. I see it. Such a little boy. Such a naked little boy.
With his pants that way. Little rat buried after he's been
made to get raped. Little boy with his asshole and his little
uncircumcised penis exposed and dry and sunken. Crawling
into himself and getting pulled out by long hands bigger
than his face. All fucked and dead and rotting and naked.
All naked in the area he should have been dropped into.
All imploded into his stunted genitalia lessons. Into his
tears for mommy and daddy and stop it and maybe it'll be
over soon and then he'll get a special treat for being so
good. You shut your fucking mouth cunt. Cunt. You shut
your fucking mouth and swallow. You shut your fucking
cunt mouth and swallow. Let me see. Let me fucking see
your cunt. Let's see your little new cunt.

G41. "When you put a rubber on and you are giving him

some head, he always said to make your mouth as tight as you can because he always liked getting young pussy."

I only told her I'd buy it. I didn't tell her what I'd do with it or how close I'd look. I know there's no such thing as a completely closed mouth. And this way I could come back. I'd have to wait 'til she offered more. And then I'd have to figure out if I was maybe being set up and if it was all going to be worth it. And when she and her biker buddies would think enough is enough and what's a scumbag like me gonna do.

G42. **1. Will you look at this photograph of the body of John Kilbride? Do you see that the trousers are pulled down below the knees, or round the knees?**

Yes. I see it. Such a little boy. Such a naked little boy. With his pants that way. Little rat buried after he's been made to get raped.

2. Just try, will you? It is obvious that there is naked skin between the knees and the thigh, save for earth that covers the flesh?

I keep looking. Only looking. I strain to see more and more from the same fucking tired veins.

3. We have been told that they were his jeans. Now look at this photograph of the body after the clothes had been removed at the mortuary. Do you see, just above the knees, there is rolled down in a roll his underpants?

I put her baby panties to my nose and detect nothing. I put it all in my mouth and suck the spit that collects around my teeth and tongue. I taste no sense of her but the knowledge that she wore them and that her parents will probably miss them.

4. It is the Prosecutions' case from those photographs, that that boy was in some way homosexually assaulted. That was something which you were ready and willing to do, was it not?

Fed a steady diet of child sexual abuse. Especially homosexual child abuse. I could see myself molesting boys very easily.

5. That is what you did to that boy on that moor or

some other place on 23 November 1963, was it not?

The boys were around and the market more defined. The boys were even aggressive. The joint was a homosexual hot-bed. All the signs on the walls are concerned with gang slogans and gang colors these days. And I'm not sure the action is still the same. It used to be all child prostitution. Teens. The boys knew who you were and what you wanted as soon as you showed up looking stupid and uncomfortable. Last time I was there it was very different. Same ages though. I'm sure I can work it out again. But I don't know how long it would take me.

6. And you buried him in that grave?

These little rats were hungry. Pronounced misfits. Little actors who were also incredibly transparent. They were burying themselves in every breath taken and sold. Young mistakes with typical pretensions, fashionably traded, and brief maladjusted histories. In fact; there was no other air to breathe than the one that all the hunting and equally hungry old perverts used to suck in and drool out.

G43. "It was in my room. I showed him a picture (of my daughter). 'Would you ever let her watch anyone do anything?' he asked. I said, 'Oh, no! My daughter don't even know what I do!'... 'Would you tell her I'm a photographer and we'll take pictures of you and she'll be comfortable... do it a couple of times, and when she gets comfortable with it, then maybe she'll take her clothes off...'"

And from Let Us Prey by Hunter Lundy, Genesis Press, 1999:

He wanted to know if she was as pretty as her picture indicated, if she had developed breasts yet, and if she had hair "down there". Murphee answered his questions and tried to change the subject.

And:

He also asked her to strike more and different poses, and again brought up the subject of her daughter. Again, she refused to discuss any involvement of her child, who was still residing with Murphee's parents in Indiana,

but she sensed that he would not let the matter drop for good.

G44. *A mother makes the trip out to the carpark where her daughter's raped and murdered body was left to garbage. She kneels down and gently places a bouquet of carefully bought flowers nearest to the spot where the body last lay. Later, she'll tell others that the long moments she spent there seeing and studying and praying among the commercial spaces and dirty utilitarian designs meant a great deal to her and her daughter's memory.*

G45. "Before I even had a dildo, he would say, 'Have you got something on the order of what you could stick in you...?'"
    I tell them to leave it alone. I can't stand that particular part.

G46. **1. Do you still want to have any contact with them?**
    I avoid them all now.
2. Would you want to work with them, e.g. as a colleague?
    Contacts were important to me back then. My thinking wasn't as clear as it should have been. It was very dangerous. It's a streamlined and tight little ugly fucking world. Where everything revolves around child abuse.
3. Would you allow them to visit you regularly as a friend?
    I see these wastes all the time. On the bus that goes through the neighborhood where I've lived the last twenty years of my life. On the street, in the bars and stores. I say hello like I do when I see the scumbags who lurch around inside these cheap backrooms I also find myself trolling. You hope there's no conversation other than the nodding politeness. That they remember where they are. That there's no place for them out in the real world.
    The start of those years were spent heavily involved in that particular pig farm. They disdain me as

214

much as I disdain them. In fact, because of my arrest, I was the more hated pariah.

4. Would you want them to be your neighbor?

They continue to live their lives the same way. I'm fairly certain that most have not been able to make things better for themselves. I ran into one of the worst of them not too long ago. He introduced me to his son. Who was about eleven.

5. Would you want to discuss your concerns and problems with them?

I don't know that it really was his son. But I had heard, through various other acquaintances, that he did get married quite a long time ago. He was very well known. I can't imagine him changing. In fact, even if he tried, there's no way he'd be able to resist the temptation. Not through all those early years of his son stretching long and slow into prepubescence and the budding teens.

6. Suppose you have children, would you allow them to take care of them, e.g. as a teacher?

I don't know how he'd be able to resist. And having him – the boy – there all the time, that life would just bend around him into something so much more vicious than anything either of us would have been able to mind or cultivate.

7. Would you allow them to look after your children, e.g. as a baby-sitter?

Trust was something that was sold at you. You, depending on what you wanted, had to pay extra for the best possible situation. And it was largely impossible to feel at ease with any single transaction. Over the years some business dealings twist into friendships but they were never firm like the ones sold in sit-coms or school books. You were always in danger and getting less than what you wanted. And, of course, what you really wanted was to be done with all of it. Just like the animals who sold it to you. Just like the animals they sold.

G47. **1. Do you like (a) boys (b) girls (c) both boys and girls?**

So many of these young boys would offer to set

you up with their girlfriends. So many of their benefactors were these old fat faggots that clearly embarrassed the boys among their friends. Some jobs were worse than others. These teens were quick to pimp anyone that wasn't their own sex. The girls would do the same.

2. At what age are they most attractive to you? (please give to nearest year)

Things have changed so much over these many years. So many of these kids look primped and faggy. They spend more time on themselves these days. The girls just seem dumb and pierced and must be pretending to get something out of it other than wretched boredom and health problems. Like a talk show appearance any day now. The boys look like they may have still been tossed out of their homes for being farmboy faggots but their wobbly mental problems seem more acceptable in loose pants and nigger colors and friends of compliant accepting mock-hoodlums.

3. What is the range of ages that you find attractive? From age___ to age___

I've lived here for so long and I've seen these wrecks take deep roots. I know how many of these diseased died during my twenties spent during the eighties. I've seen them go home to mom and step-dad on TV and, honestly, I've seen a rough trade sensitive type, that I used to know somewhat well, turn up sold and slaughtered into pieces stuffed into the bottom of a dumpster. So many of these cunts had AIDS back then. So many paid in badly cut rat poison. So many of these white trash uptown skinnies got it handed back to them in spades.

4. What is it about children that attracts you?

Some of these delinquents rotate into the garbage that do the same as I did and I've watched some end up on the gay side of charity food delivery jobs and the wrong side of peep show trolls.

And even if I didn't recognize them anymore. Or they me. And even if I'm completely wrong about who these mouths and speedy fingers and tattooed backs are: It's still all the same.

5. How do you view the idea of sex with adults?

*I wish I had photographs of these stretching pits.
Them with their girlfriends. The way they were to remind
me of what they are now. Nothing illegal. Mostly with
their clothes on.*

**6. What were your parents like, and how did you ever
get on with them? (a) Your mother (b) Your father.**

*Close-ups of their faces and the acne and wide
wet mouths and protruding dark red lips. Their dull eyes
and low brows and deep set problems and poses.*

7. What was their attitude towards sex?

*There is no need to make it anything other than
what it is. A photograph taken of a hustler standing
wherever he'd like to stand. Nothing homo sinister in the
background. It doesn't have to be in front of the arcade
that's still there on Belmont. Or in one of the alleys behind
the restaurant grease traps or lake-side tearooms.*

*I'm looking at the mouth that he used for
anything other than sucking cock or selling what little he
could get.*

**8. Describe the earliest sexual experience you can
remember.**

*What's the difference between your breath and
the nigger hookers' breath on Lake Street?*

**9. What kinds of relationships have you had with
children?**

*Others would do the more blunt desperate acts
and I'd be happy to buy it from them. But for me; I'd just
want something other than the obvious sentimental or
lustful recollections. I wouldn't want to turn it into your
stupid idea of human. The fag collectors would tell them:*

Take your shirt off.

Get your cock hard.

Do you think you could cum?

*Let me see the muscles in your ass. Turn around
again. Don't smile.*

Spread your asscheeks apart farther.

Lean back against the wall.

I want to catch the drip.

**10. Do you have fantasies concerning relationships
with children? If so, what kind and how often?**

As you age, the idea that a biology that would force you to answer against your will tends to seep away into nothing. The lies about mistakes and fumblings, about lessons and instinct, about warm memories and dirty comforting fixations are no longer necessary. Not for yourself or your parents and probation officers. You try and recall what you need to know and little else. Until you're forced by regret and threat and financial destruction into remembering exactly how unimportant it all is.

The kids start hating you after awhile. Not without good reason. And it becomes still more dangerous.

11. What would you like to do with children if legal restrictions were entirely removed?

The best fuck I ever had came twenty years after I did it. I knew he was sexually and neglectfully abused and I watched him knot up into a helpless young waste. His mental capacity degenerated severely over these years with or without any very small degree of help from me.

12. How do you feel about your preference for children? Are you puzzled, happy, disturbed, or what?

Too many people suddenly had pictures. The prices, because I always bought them, had started to rise. I was that much of a sucker. I had been promised much more but it was merely a carrot dangled in front of me so that I would try and keep my dealers happy by buying every single inferior item they ever offered me.

13. Have you ever sought professional advice or treatment? If so, from what kind of person or institution?

I had asked others. And the price was always too much. I simply didn't have enough money. I would have gotten into more serious trouble if I had the money they wanted me to spend.

14. Is there anything else you wish to say about your paedophile interests or behavior?

The hard shell boy in the dumpster was the most sensational but it wasn't the best or the worst case I remember. The one I remember crawling and crying at me. Him begging me to help him and then apologizing the very next minute and then breaking into fierce, absolutely

frightening, tears again the minute after that. He doesn't seem the most remarkable either. Not after all these years.

15. Would you be willing to be interviewed in person by this researcher on the understanding that confidentiality would be maintained? If so, please give a contact address or phone number.

Nothing matters if it starts confidential. The questions are almost always going to be more truthful than the answers. Until you put a face and a name and a photograph to them.

G48. *He had turned paranoid. He kept asking me not to hurt him anymore. I hadn't. I told him I never meant to. He was so much younger than me then. He was out of his burning fractured mind on a bad mix of constant drugs and alcohol and bad ageing sex. I hugged him and he responded. I gave him the rest of the money I had and told him it was all I had.*

G49. *You could kiss the boys. Faggots do that. You don't kiss nigger-lipped nigger whores. The same way you don't pay them to piss on you. Neither of you should enjoy it.*

G50. *I get an erection whenever anyone cries. I've been that way since I was a kid.*

G51. *I had to leave that particular situation. It had all the earmarks of a potential attack or a loud neighborhood investigation or a second class x felony arrest. I told him it was OK. That he needed some rest. I would take him back to his friends who loved him and who would help him get through this only one bad night. He had put his tongue in my mouth. I told him not to worry about it. He was a few months away from suicide. I wasn't sure until then that he was really suffering or if he was just fucking with me for laughs or more money.*

G52. *Ten-year-old Pamela Butler was snatched off the street she was rollerblading on and stuffed into Keith Nelson's truck. Her handwritten missing poster listed her as*

wearing a sports bra. Similarly aged Gina North is seen running towards whoever is manning the camera – her mother, father, friend, someone close. She was playing in someone's backyard and her small skinny body is soaked from a sprinkler or a pool or something like that. An orange top wet and clung tight to her chest, cut above her firm thin stomach down to her tiny blue slick panties. A dark wet blue bikini bottom tied high on her long juvenile thighs. Long blonde matted hair and she sticks her tongue out.

G53. It is possible that there is some great form of inexplicable grief that allows or forces these ruptured mothers and fathers to give out their old home movies and personal photographs. Something must have gone wrong. Something unfair. A terrible crack in the plan. And there must be some relief found in crying and sharing and growing up to know it. I just haven't made it yet. Creeps like me don't get it. But. For now. They simply must be telling the truth.